The GolfBook for Kids

A Great Learning Tool for Young Golfers or New Golfers of Any Age

Jim Corbett   and   **Chris Aoki**
Mr. Golf Etiquette   **PGA Professional**

Illustrations: Art Penn Studios
Photography: Mike Helmuth

HARA
PUBLISHING GROUP

Published by
Hara Publishing
P.O. Box 19732
Seattle, WA 98109

ISBN: 1-883697-87-5

Library of Congress Catalog Card Number:
00-103882

Manufactured in the United States
10 9 8 7 6 5 4 3 2

Cover Design: Scott Fisher
Cover Photography: Jim Corbett
Editor: Victoria McCown
Book Design & Production: Scott and Shirley Fisher
Illustrations: Art Penn Studios
Photography: Mike Helmuth

Table of Contents

Authors' Dedications

This book is dedicated to the other members of my life's foursome: my wife, Tami, my daughter, Cadie, and my son, Jeffrey, without whose love and support this book would not have been completed and my life wouldn't be nearly as much fun.

— Jim Corbett

This book is dedicated to my father, Min Aoki, who taught me many valuable lessons in golf and in life. I am grateful to have learned from him his love of golf.

— Chris Aoki

Acknowledgments

The authors would like to extend a heartfelt thank you to those who assisted in the creation of this book: Nick Arakaki, Erika Cole, Cadie Corbett, Jeffrey Corbett, Bradi Haggett and Tyler Haggett for portraying the best in young golfers in our photographs; Bob Brown of "Keepers of the Game," at www.keepers.org. Jim Hofmeister, and Kirk Smith for their good advice; Harbour Pointe Golf Club in Mukilteo, Washington, for use of their facilities; and Henry-Griffitts, Inc. for use of their equipment.

Thanks also to the friendly golfers whose pictures adorn the front and back covers of The GolfBook for Kids: (cover) Paris Schmidt, Danny Kitt, Benjamin Shiau, Anna Karlsen, Jeffery Corbett and Cadie Corbett; (back) Rob Townsend, Andrew (AJ) Townsend and Nicholas (Cole) Townsend.

About the Authors

Jim Corbett is the creator and developer of the award-winning web site, "Mr. Golf Etiquette," at www.mrgolf.com. Mr. Corbett is a regular guest on the Golf Guys Radio Show, nationally broadcast out of Monterey, California, where he discusses the important issues of golf etiquette.

Jim is the Vice President of Business Development at VersusLaw, Inc. (www.versuslaw.com), an Internet-based legal research service in Redmond, Washington.

Jim began playing golf almost thirty years ago when, as a young boy, he caddied at a public golf course. He is now an avid golfer who plays as often as his schedule allows, which is not nearly enough.

About the Authors

Chris Aoki, a PGA teaching professional, has been involved in teaching golf for over twenty years and currently runs the Chris Aoki Golf Schools at Harbour Pointe Golf Club in Mukilteo, Washington. She welcomes students of all ages and skill levels.

Her success and reputation as one of the best golf instructors for young players is due to her methods of teaching the golf swing as an understandable process and her ability to convey that clearly in terms that kids can comprehend.

She is a Masterfitter™ for Henry-Griffitts, Inc. and has developed a method of fitting putters used by instructors across the U.S. who fit Henry-Griffitts TotalTest™ Fit² Aim™ Putters. She has been invited to teach the golf swing and club fitting to coaches and golf professionals throughout the United States, Canada, and Australia.

Her website is www.aokigolf.com

Authors' Notes

The GolfBook for Kids was written to be an introductory book on golf for kids and all "kids at heart." Throughout the text you will see that the instructions and the photographs all relate to kids. But people of all ages are learning to enjoy the game of golf, so the authors want to be sure that if you fall more into that "kids at heart" category, you remember to approach learning the game in the same way a kid would.

When kids learn a new game they focus on having fun. They are not worried about how they look or even if they are doing it "right." If it's fun, they'll do it over and over and before you know it they're getting really good. If you approach golf with the enthusiasm and positive attitude of a kid and you leave the burdens of the grown-up world behind, you will have a lifetime of enjoyment playing one of the most wonderful games the world has ever known.

In order to help parents in guiding young golfers, the authors have included some *Practice Tips*, some *Parent's Notes* and some *Safety Tips*.

Practice Tips are marked by a bucket of balls.

Parent's Notes/Safety Tips are marked by a green with a flag.

Words that are in **bold** are defined in the glossary at the back of the book.

Best of luck and enjoy the great game of golf!

Jim Corbett
Chris Aoki

Foreword

The game of golf has had a very positive impact on my life. In addition to earning my living as a professional golfer there are many important lessons about life that I have learned from playing golf. I have learned the importance of patience, humility, personal integrity and sportsmanship.

Golf teaches patience because no one can learn it all right away. It takes a lot of practice to learn to play well. The game continually teaches humility because just when you think you know how to do it perfectly it is possible to lose your game altogether.

Golf is a game of personal integrity because you keep your own score and call the penalty shots on yourself. You soon realize that there is no point in fudging the score because the only one who gets cheated is yourself. And the sportsmanship and etiquette of golf are a part of the tradition as old as the game itself.

I learned to play golf as a kid. I enjoyed it from the beginning, but the adults who encouraged me and supported my efforts, helped to make the game a special part of my life. I think *The GolfBook for Kids* can get kids (or parents who are helping their children) started in the right direction with the right attitude about the game of golf.

Golf is a game that is fun, challenging and richly rewarding in many ways. And if you start practicing when you are young and you enjoy the game as much as I did, maybe we'll see your name on a leader board at some time in the future.

Keep 'em in the fairway!

All the best,

Juli Inkster

Juli Inkster ranks among the most successful golfers in the history of the game. Beginning with her three consecutive U.S. Amateur Championships (1980-82), and her 1984 LPGA Rookie of the Year award, through her remarkable 1999 season on the LPGA Tour when she won the U.S. Open and the LPGA Championship, Juli has been well-loved and respected for her contributions to the game. Juli is also admired for her ability to balance the needs of her family (husband, Brian, and daughters, Hayley and Cori) with the demands of a competitive touring schedule.

Juli Inkster is a Year 2000 inductee into the LPGA Hall of Fame.

Introduction

Golf is a hit! All over the world more and more kids are learning to play golf -- and loving it!

Among other things, the exciting emergence of Tiger Woods -- first through his amateur years and then his captivating debut as a professional has ignited a spark. That spark has fired up the interest of kids to play golf and even to coax their parents into playing too!

The GolfBook for Kids provides young golfers with a look at the entire game of golf so they can understand not only how to play, but how the elements of the game make golf unique among sports. The tradition, the golf clubs, the technique of the swing are a few examples.

The GolfBook for Kids introduces new golfers, from about five years old and up, and their families to a game that will inspire a lifetime of enjoyment together. (Note: it is assumed that golfers under ten years old will work closely with a parent/coach.) In **The GolfBook for Kids** you will learn how to play the game and how to keep score accurately. By understanding how golf clubs are designed and how they help you send the ball flying through the air, you will learn to make all the important golf shots.

Most of all **The GolfBook for Kids** will teach you to play the game, carrying with you the rich heritage of courtesies golfers extend to one another. This code of courtesy is known as golf etiquette.

xi

When you practice good golf etiquette, your example will be passed to your fellow golfers as others have passed it on for centuries before you. Play golf with love and respect for the game and you will become a part of the tradition that goes all the way back to the links of Scotland. And remember what the word "golf" stands for: Go Outfer Lotsa Fun!

Well, maybe that's NOT what it REALLY stands for, but that's what you can think of when you play. So let's get started on a lifetime of fun playing golf!

Welcome to the Ancient Game of Golf

Lost in the Mists of Time

Long, long ago in Scotland, on a windswept meadow that rolled gently down to the sea, a pair of lonely shepherds watched over their flock. Using their long shepherd's crooks to guide the sheep, they took their flock to the best places for forage. With their faithful dog to protect them, they wandered the sandy terrain covered in rich grasses. The land they traveled seemed to link the sea itself to the firmer ground farther inland and to the mountains beyond.

As they traversed the hills, their spirits were uplifted by the beauty of their surroundings. The brisk breeze off the ocean rustled through the long seaside grass and wildflowers. Every now and then a hawk flew overhead or a little rabbit scurried about in the bushes.

One day, in an effort to alleviate the boredom of a long afternoon, one of the shepherds turned to the other and said, "MacDuff, aye'll bet ye a boowl o' steamin' Haggis and a pint of yerrr finest ale tha' aye kin smock this wee rrrock into th' rrrabbit hoole tha' ye kin see strrraight 'way, in fewerrr trrries than ye kin dooit."

Long ago, on the windy linksland of Scotland,
a couple of shepherds played a game...

MacDuff looked up at him with a strange look on his face and said, "Huh?" After the first shepherd explained what he was talking about, MacDuff focused his good eye on the entrance to the little rabbit den which was about fifty yards away. He puffed up his burly chest and told his partner, "Ye got yerrrself a bet therrr, Hackerrr. Ye know full well therrre's nae a Hackerrr in the valley tha' kin best a MacDuff at any game ye can play!"

With a mighty whack from the curved end of his staff Hacker sent his little stone sailing toward the rabbit hole. It landed about half way to the target and he was quite satisfied with his effort. He turned to his playing partner, grinned and winked.

MacDuff stood at about the same spot and eyed his little stone sitting on the sandy ground. He took several practice swings and got himself ready. He checked the wind and lined up his shot again. He used his foot to pat down the area behind his ball so he could make better contact and studied his stone for a long minute.

Hacker finally shouted, "C'mon, man, ye'rrre takin' all day. Joost hit the thing and be doone wi' it!" MacDuff took a powerful, lunging swing. Unfortunately, just as he swung a little sheep ran right behind him and startled him with a little "Bahhh" and MacDuff sent his stone flying way off to the right!

He yelled at the lamb as he watched his stone sail in the wrong direction and he called to his dog, "Get it, Mulligan! Tha's it, booy, brrring it bock." When the dog dutifully returned with the stone, and dropped it into his master's hand, MacDuff said, "Goood booy, aye'll take tha', Mulligan." And he turned to Hacker with a sheepish grin (after all, he WAS a shepherd!) and said, "Well, maybe aye'll just trrry tha' 'un agin."

The Game Grows and Grows

From that humble beginning on the sunny **linksland** by the sea, the game of golf was born. Soon all the shepherds were trying their luck at the game and before long the people in the towns and villages were also entertaining themselves by whacking stones into rabbit holes across the countryside.

By the early 1400s the city of St. Andrew's on the east coast of Scotland had become a regional golfing center. It had a course that once included 22 holes. Later that course was reduced to 18 holes and from that time forward the standard for golf courses worldwide has been the same -- 18 holes.

While the original shepherds had used stones in their contests, people now used hard wooden balls and later they would make golf balls out of small leather pouches packed with feathers. The first shepherd's staffs were also replaced with clubs

3

that were manufactured by the bow and arrow makers of the village.

As the popularity of the game spread even the nobles of Scotland and their soldiers found the game to be a delight. In fact, they were devoting so much time to playing golf that in 1457 the King of Scotland forbade his subjects to play anymore. He felt they were spending more time playing golf than practicing their archery skills.

Archery, of course, was very important because that was their main means of defending their country from England. But some years later, after a peace treaty had been signed, it once again became acceptable to play golf and then even the kings and queens themselves began to enjoy the game.

Mary, Queen of Scots, enjoyed the game so much that when her husband died in 1567, she went out to play a round of golf the very next day. She was sharply criticized for appearing to have fun at a time when she should be in mourning. "Mourning?" she cried, "You bet I'm in mourning! I just four-putted the sixteenth hole!" (Or something to that effect).

Structure Is Brought to the Game

Local tournaments were formed so men and women could compete to see who was the best golfer in a town or county. But since there were so many different areas where golf was played, it was deemed necessary to draw up a standard set of rules by which all golfers could play. In 1744 a group of golfers in Edinburgh did just that and created the "Articles and Laws in Playing the Golf."

The original rules instructed golfers what to do in case "...your ball come among any watery filth" (take a stroke and "throw it behind the hazard six yards at least"). They also let golfers know that if during a swing "...your club should break in any way, it is accounted as a stroke."

Those original rules also included many still in effect today, almost exactly as they were written then: "He whose ball lyes furthest from the hole is obliged to play first" and "If a ball is stop'd by any person, horse, dog or anything else, the ball so stop'd must be played where it lyes."

A Game of Honor

Golf has always been a game that has placed a strong emphasis on adhering to the rules and on personal honor. Golfers keep their own scores and if penalties are called, golfers generally call them on themselves. This code of honesty has long been a part of the game of golf and there are have been instances in which players have lost tournaments because of penalty strokes they called on themselves.

No instance of personal integrity is more vivid in the minds of golfers than the story of a man named Bobby Jones. As a young boy, Bobby Jones showed an unusual knack for the game of golf. He was able to beat many of the professional golfers of his day even when he was just in his teens. In the 1920s he had won many of the most prestigious golf tournaments in the world, and even though he was competing against professionals he always played as an amateur (which means he never accepted the prize money).

In the U.S. Open in 1925 Bobby gave himself a one stroke penalty because, as he got ready to hit his ball which was sitting in some long grass, the ball moved. No one else had seen the ball move, but Jones respected the game and the rules so much that he insisted on giving himself the penalty stroke.

Because of that penalty he tied for the lead in the tournament instead of winning it. He lost the next day in a play-off. Even though he eventually won four U.S. Open titles, because of that loss he was prevented from winning a fifth title — something no one has ever done.

When he was later commended for his honesty, he brushed it off, saying, "There is only one way to play the game. You might as well praise a man for not robbing a bank." Many amateur and professional golfers still hold Bobby Jones in the highest esteem because of how he played the game and how he lived his life.

A Game for the Whole World

Golf is a game that can be played and enjoyed at every level of ability. In addition to the purely recreational games that are played every day, there are tournaments of all kinds that players enjoy as well. Of course, there are the well-known professional tournaments that can be viewed on TV, but there are also lots of local tournaments and junior tournaments in which you can participate if you learn to play and if you love to play!

The game of golf is enjoyed around the world by people of all ages and from all walks of life; from Europe to North America to Asia and from Australia to South America to Africa, the game of golf is played. Wherever you travel, be sure to bring your clubs because you are likely to find a great place to play.

Started by shepherds on a grassy hill overlooking the sea in Scotland and transported around the world by people who love the game, golf continues to grow in popularity. The history of golf is a story of professional players who are very skilled at the game as well as a story of average players who simply love the game. Remember when you swing your clubs that you are a part of the history of the game and it is up to you to keep the game as wonderful as it has always been!

From Scotland the game of golf was exported to the whole world.

Little did those shepherds realize the impact they would have on the world as a result of that simple game they played. The game they created has indeed grown and developed into a sport that is played and loved the world over — it is the great game of golf!

Learn it! Play it! Love it!

Chapter 2

The Golf Course — Playing in the Great Outdoors

The first golf courses were formed completely by nature; the sea and the wind sculpted the terrain and the game was shaped to fit the land. Since the very beginning, golfers have been drawn to the game by the natural beauty of the environment in which it is played.

Golf courses today are designed to blend with their natural settings and to highlight the beauty of the surroundings. Whether the game is played on a desert course, a course in the mountains, or a seaside course, golfers have a feeling of peaceful appreciation to be playing in the great outdoors.

In most other sports, such as soccer, football, hockey, or basketball, the playing area is exactly the same no matter where you play. The distance between the bases is always the same, the height and width of the goal mouth is always the same, the amount of yardage for a first down is always the same and the height of the net is always the same. But in golf, the courses are all different, the designs of the **holes** are all different, the playing conditions are all different, and so the game is always new and different.

(In golf, the word "hole" can have two meanings: one meaning is for the actual hole in the ground into which you will hit your ball; the other meaning describes the entire distance from the **teeing ground** all the way to the **green**, as in "the eighteenth hole.")

Par for the Course

The holes on a golf course are all different distances. They are organized according to the score of **par**, which is the score an expert golfer would be expected to make on a given hole. The shorter holes (up to 250 yards) are par 3's; the middle distance holes (between 250 yards and 470 yards) are par 4's; and the long holes (over 470 yards) are par 5's.

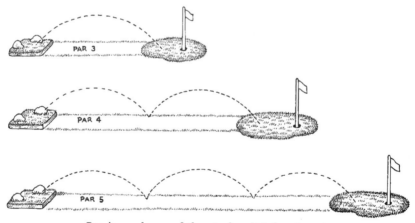

Par is made up of the strokes it takes to get onto the green plus two putts.

The score of par assumes a golfer will take two putts on each hole. So, when trying to get par on a par-3 hole, a golfer tries to get the ball onto the green in one shot, leaving two putts to make par. On a par-4, a golfer will try to get onto the green in two shots, with two putts for par and on a par-5, three strokes are given to get on, with two putts for par. Landing on the green in the designated number of strokes, not counting the two putts, is referred to as **getting on in regulation**.

Sometimes it is possible to get the ball into the hole in fewer strokes than par. When that happens, it's a GOOD thing. One stroke under par is called a **birdie**. Two strokes under par is called an **eagle**. (An eagle is a really BIG birdie!) There is also the double-eagle, or three strokes under par. A double-eagle is one of the rarest scores in golf, but it has been done! And of course, there is the **hole-in-one**, which is getting the ball into the hole in one stroke.

A score of one stroke over par is called a **bogey**. There are bogeys, double bogeys, triple bogeys, and so on up the line. Try not to let the number in front of the word bogey get too high!

The Layout

Even though every golf course is different in design and terrain, every golf course contains similar elements. The illustration below shows the basic components of a course, but these components can come in an infinite variety of combinations.

The course consists of two main places where you want your ball to go and a whole lot of places where you don't want your ball to go. The places where you DO want the ball to go from the teeing ground (most often simply referred to as the **tee**), are the **fairway**, and the green. If you can keep your ball in those places, golf will always be fun — and your score will be a lot better!

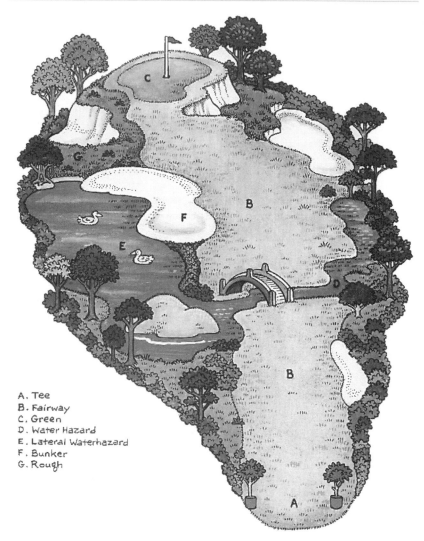

A. Tee
B. Fairway
C. Green
D. Water Hazard
E. Lateral Waterhazard
F. Bunker
G. Rough

The first golf courses were created by nature; modern courses are enhanced by natural beauty.

However, you will see there are other places where your ball might go. These are places like the **rough**, or the **hazards**. If you spend too much time visiting those areas of the golf course, you may find the game a bit more challenging.

12

For now, let's look at some of the parts of the golf course, how they fit in the game, and how they make golf unique among sports. As the March Hare in *Alice in Wonderland* said, "Begin at the beginning ... and go on till you come to the end: then stop." So let's begin at the beginning — and the beginning of a game of golf is at the teeing ground.

The Teeing Ground

Golfers hit their first shot on a hole from the teeing ground, which we have shortened to "tee." When you arrive at the tee you will see two markers on the ground spread a few yards apart. Those markers designate the area from which you will first hit the ball.

When it is your turn to hit, find a nice level spot between the markers. You can put the ball anywhere you choose between the markers and as far back from the markers as the length of two clubs. However, you may not place your ball in front of the markers. That area between the markers and back two club lengths is the official teeing ground.

The teeing ground is from the front of the markers, back two club lengths.

Most courses provide at least three sets of tees from which players can choose: the forward tees, the middle tees and the back tees. If you are a new golfer, you may want to play from the forward tees.

Here you see the forward, middle, and back tees.

The Fairway

After you hit the ball from the tee, the laws of gravity ensure that it will come down somewhere. If your shot from the tee was a good one and went where you aimed, your ball probably landed in the fairway. The fairway is a great place to be. The grass is mowed short and even and your ball will sit up very nicely, giving you a good **lie** for your next shot.

The length and width of the fairways varies quite a bit. On some holes the fairway will be long, wide, and straight; others could be more narrow with sharp turns so that you can't even see where the green is from your second shot. When a fairway

The Golf Course — Playing The Great Outdoors

has a bend in it, golfers refer to that bend as a **dogleg**. You will often hear golfers refer to a dogleg right or a dogleg left. That means the fairway bends to the right or left and, viewed from above, that bend resembles the back leg of a dog.

Looking around while you are in the fairway, you will notice several markers that tell you how far it is to your ultimate destination — the green. One of the most common markers indicates the distance of 150 yards from the green, and it often comes in the shape of a bush or a small tree.

The 150-yard marker measures the distance to the middle of the green.

On some courses yardage markers along the fairway show where the distance is 250 yards, 200 yards, 150 yards, and 100 yards to the green. In many instances these yardage markers can be found on the sprinkler heads around the fairway.

These markers help you to gauge how far you are from the hole and therefore which club you should use. For instance, if you know you can hit your 5-iron 150 yards and your ball is right near the 150-yard marker, you know to use that club.

When you hit your ball from the fairway, your club will often take out a piece of grass and dirt with the shot. This chunk of stuff is called a **divot**. After you watch where your ball lands, replace the divot and press it down with your foot, or fill the hole with the sand and seed mixture provided by the

course. **Replacing your divot** (or filling the divot hole) will
allow the grass
to grow back
and will keep
the golf course
in the best pos-
sible condition
for the future.
(We'll talk more
about this in
the chapter on
golf etiquette.)

*Careful and considerate golfers will always
repair their divots.*

The Green

After you have taken your shot (or shots) from the fairway,
the ball will eventually land on the green. The green is a very
special place for golfers; it is here that you take some of the
most important shots in the game.

The grass surface of the green is cut quite short and is very
smooth. Because the green requires a lot of work by the greens
crew to keep the grass on the green healthy, it is important
for all golfers to treat the green with care and respect. When
golfers are on the green they walk slowly. They don't make
marks on the green with their shoes or their clubs.

You will also notice that the green is not flat; there are
places where it rolls in little hills and mounds and even some
places where it dips quite a bit. Those dips and turns will alter
the course of your golf ball on its way to the hole. As you learn
the fine art of putting, you will learn how to **read the green;**
that is, you will figure out how to putt so your ball goes along
the correct line, right into the hole!

Greens are rarely flat and level — sometimes they even have two tiers.

Situated on the green is the hole with the tall flagstick. The flagstick has a little knob that holds it in the bottom of the hole. The greens crew will change the location of the hole every day for two reasons: 1) so the hole plays differently every day, and 2) so the grass is not continually worn down in one spot on the green.

When you are on the green, you will mainly use your putter to tap the ball to the hole, hopefully in one or two strokes.

The Rough

Along each side of the fairway is an area that is made up of grass that is longer than the grass in the fairway. And depend-ing on the part of the country in which you play golf, you may find it full of bushes, rocks, weeds, sawgrass, thistles, and lions and tigers and bears. Oh, my! This area is called the **rough**.

If your ball lands in the rough, the first problem you may have is finding it. Since the grass and other stuff you encoun-ter in the rough is long and thick and sometimes wet and snarly, your golf ball can very easily settle into it in a way

The long grass and uneven footing of the rough can make for a challenging shot.

that makes it difficult to locate. And then, once you DO find your ball, you face the challenge of hitting it out.

It isn't easy to hit out of wet, snarly stuff — hey, that's why they call it the rough! Sometimes the best strategy is to simply take a highly lofted club and hit the ball back out into the fairway to give yourself a decent lie and begin again from there.

Hazards

The golf course is full of hazards that make the game much more interesting. Of course, when it's *your* ball that lands in the hazard, it loses much of its appeal.

There are two main types of hazards that are defined in the Rules of Golf, bunkers and water hazards.

Bunkers

Bunkers can best be described as pits, usually filled with sand deliberately placed on the golf course. Some golfers refer to bunkers as **sand traps**, but the only term used in the Rules of Golf to describe them is bunkers, so it's probably a good idea to call them by that name. They are a remnant of the days when golf was played on the sandy, grassy linksland of old Scotland.

Bunkers come in a wide variety of shapes and sizes and can be filled with different types of sand. You may find bunkers located anywhere on the course including right next to the greens or out in the fairways. Some are shallow, almost level with the fairway, while others are deep with high walls that require special shots to get over the edge.

Water Hazards

A **water hazard** is a body of water on or next to the course. It could be an ocean, a lake, a stream, a river, a marsh, or a drainage ditch. When your ball goes into a water hazard, your best option is to drop a ball behind the water hazard along a straight line from the hole to where your ball crossed into the hazard. (We'll cover other options in the discussion on rules.)

Water hazards are marked with **yellow stakes** or yellow lines.

Water hazards usually run across the fairway.

Lateral Water Hazards

A **lateral water hazard** is a water hazard, or part of a water hazard, that is situated in a way that does not allow you to easily drop a ball behind it on a line between the hole and the place where the ball went into the hazard. Usually your best choice is to drop a ball to the side of the hazard exactly where the ball entered the hazard, but no nearer to the hole.

Lateral water hazards are marked with **red stakes** or red lines.

Red stakes mark the lateral water hazard.

Out of Bounds

There is one other area that you should try to avoid during your game of golf, and that is the area referred to as **out of bounds**. Out of bounds is marked with **white stakes**, white lines, or boundary fences and runs in various places along the perimeter of a hole or the course.

This golfer narrowly escaped going out of bounds.

Through the Green

As you play golf and read books about golf, you will hear the expression **through the green**, which refers to any part of the course except the teeing ground, the green to which you are playing, and all hazards on the course. It is important to understand the term because sometimes rules are based on whether your ball is "through the green" or in a hazard.

Local Variations

Some courses include areas that are environmentally sensitive or have homes not far from the fairway. In these instances there may be some local course rules that protect these areas.

Summary

Some people think that golfers play their game against the course, that the course holds all the challenges and you must conquer the course in order to win. That is not true. If you understand and appreciate the golf course, you will learn that you play your game in harmony with the golf course.

Golf courses are beautiful places. There is a wonderful variety of plants and animals that live on the course and spending time there is relaxing and enjoyable. Always be sure to take care of the course and treat it with respect. Countless others will play the course after you, and they are entitled to the same beautiful environment you experienced. It is your responsibility to leave the course the same way you found it.

Chapter 3

Golf Equipment — It's in the Bag!

One of the things you will quickly learn when you take up the game of golf is that there is no shortage of "stuff" to buy. There are all kinds of gadgets and gizmos and gear on which the unwary new golfer can spend money. But most of that stuff is not necessary and doesn't really help you learn to play the game any better.

In order to play a game of golf, however, some equipment is absolutely necessary and other equipment is optional. For instance, most golf courses have a mandatory rule that each golfer must play with his or her own set of golf clubs and golf bag, a rule that helps to move the game along. And of course, having plenty of extra golf balls and tees is a good idea for every golfer.

Let's look at some of the equipment that golfers use, how it works, and why it's important to your game.

Your Golf Bag

Golf bags come in many sizes, colors, and styles. Some are designed to be lightweight so you can carry your golf clubs; others, like the one

Golf bags come in lots of different sizes and styles.

in the photo, are designed for golf carts that you ride with your golf bag strapped onto the back.

One advantage of a larger golf bag is the extra pockets where you can store all the stuff that you will need during your round of golf. In addition to clubs and balls, which will be discussed shortly, here are a few things you may want to bring along in your golf bag:

- A bottle of water or soft drink
- Something to snack on (a sandwich or some snack bars)
- Some band-aids (in case you get a blister on your foot)
- Sunscreen (if it's hot)
- Rain gear (if it's not)
- A jacket or sweatshirt
- A golf towel
- A copy of this book!

The only time you might have a problem bringing a lot of stuff in your bag is when a **caddie** carries it for you! A caddie is a person you can hire to carry your golf bag during a round of golf, and if you get a caddie with lots of experience, it can be a worthwhile expense. A good caddie can tell you the exact distances from wherever your ball is to the green, point out trouble spots and give you savvy advice on how to play the course.

If you live near a good golf course, you may have a chance to work as a caddie at some point. If so, take advantage of it. It's a great way to learn the game of golf and some golf courses let caddies play for free during certain times.

Now that you've loaded just about everything you own into your golf bag, check to see if you left any room for your golf clubs and balls!

Golf Balls

The **golf ball** is probably the most basic piece of equipment in the game of golf. After all, without the ball there really is no game.

As was mentioned in the introduction, the very first golfers probably used stones in their contests, but as the game grew in popularity other materials were soon substituted. For a long time golfers used leather balls stuffed with feathers. (The proper measurement was a top hat full of feathers hand-stuffed into a little leather casing.) Those balls were expensive because they had to be individually made, and they were difficult to hit well.

Around the middle of the 1800s, a method was found to make golf balls out of hard rubber. Then in the early 1900s the modern golf ball was developed. Today golf balls are constructed in different ways (solid center, wound center, two piece, three piece, etc.); but the thing that has made the modern golf ball so much better than anything that came before it is the pattern of **dimples** that you see around the ball.

The dimples help give the ball "lift" and control its direction. When struck by a club, the ball actually spins backwards as it flies through the air. And, just like the wing of an airplane is designed to channel airflow and give the plane

lift, the dimples on the golf ball channel air over and under it, adding lift
to its trajectory.

And, of course, by keeping the ball
up in the air longer, you will get
greater distance in your shot.

There are hundreds of brands of golf
balls from which you can choose. Some
golf balls are designed to give you more
spin, some to provide greater distance.
Basically, all of them are pretty good.
But the most important thing to remember when you choose a brand of
golf balls is this: Don't choose the one
with the hat full of feathers!

*There are many brands
of golf balls and they all
work pretty well — if
you hit them right!*

Golf Clubs

According to the Rules of Golf, a golfer is allowed to have up
to fourteen clubs in his or her bag during a round of golf.
Which clubs you choose to play with is an important decision
and will obviously have a big impact on your game. Your clubs
should be fitted to you in their length, shaft flex, lie angle,
and the size of the grip. (For a full explanation, see the
appendix on club fitting.) The clubs should be matched to one
another so they will feel the same no matter what club you
are using.

There are three basic categories of clubs: **woods**, **irons**, and
putters. Each has different characteristics that create different patterns of ball flight or roll, depending on the situation.
The woods and irons are "full swing" clubs, which simply means
that when you hit them, you generally take a full swing at the
ball. The putter is used on the green to roll the ball directly to
the hole.

Golf clubs are designed and engineered so the golfer can use a consistent swing and still get very different results (mainly in loft and distance) from the various clubs.

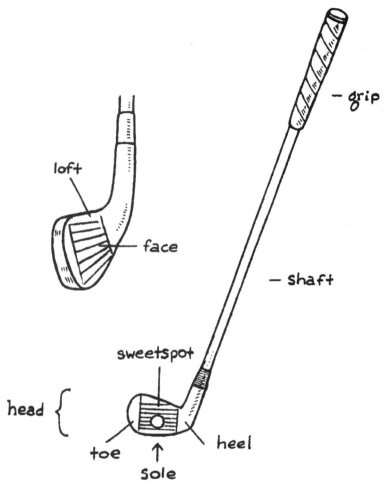

The club pictured here is an iron, but on irons, woods, and putters, the parts have the same names.

The golf club **grip** is a piece of material fitted around the shaft of the club to provide a comfortable place to hold it.

Many years ago leather was used to make the grip. Today certain types of rubber are more common. Different golfers like different kinds of grips: Some like a tacky, stickier feel and others like a rougher-feeling grip. The idea is to increase the comfort of holding the golf club with less tension. Grips should be kept clean and replaced at a golf shop if they become slippery or worn.

The **shaft** of the golf club can be made of different materials. Many golf club shafts are made of slightly flexible steel; others are made from a lighter material called graphite which is also quite flexible. The flex in the shaft helps kick the ball into the air and give it height and distance.

The **head** of the golf club is usually made of metal. The bottom of the club is called the **sole** and it is designed to glide through the grass. The flat, sloping part of the head that hits the ball is called the **face**. The outer part of the face is called the toe of the club and the inner part of the face is called the **heel**. So there is a toe and a heel on the face! Aren't you glad people don't look like that?

When the clubface strikes the golf ball, the ball compresses, or flattens, and rebounds in the direction the clubface is pointing. The most solid part of the face — the place where you want to hit the ball on the grooves — is called the **sweet spot**. It is typically located at the lower center of the face.

Full Swing Clubs (Woods and Irons)

The two styles of full swing golf clubs, woods and irons are similar in that they both have grips, shafts, clubheads (although they are designed differently), clubfaces, and grooves. The principle of how they work is the same. The main and most obvious difference is that the woods have a much bigger head and are designed to send the ball longer distances.

The length of the shaft and the loft of the face are different for each wood in the set.

The head sizes are also different. From left to right, 1 (driver), 3, 5 and 7 woods.

Why are woods called "woods" when they are made of metal? Originally all golf clubs were made by hand from very hard wood. As the game evolved, club makers started using various metals to make the clubs harder and stronger. The clubs that were first made from metals became know as "irons."

The clubs with the larger heads were still made from very hard wood (usually persimmon) until about the 1970s and those clubs were referred to as the "woods." Now, with improved technology, most woods are actually made of metal, too, so they can be weighted and designed with more versatility and consistency. But even though they are most often made of metal, the name "woods" has stuck with them. Some woods are still made of wood, but it is becoming more and more uncommon.

Golf clubs have become specialized for specific tasks. Clubs have different lengths and the faces of the clubs are set to different angles. Clubs with steeper angles, or more **loft**, will send the ball higher into the air, but for a shorter distance. The clubs with less of an angle, or less loft, will send the ball on a lower trajectory, but for a greater distance.

The different lofts help you create different shots with your clubs.

You will also see on your own clubs that they are all numbered (a typical set of irons includes a 3-iron to a 9-iron,

The higher the number, the greater the loft of the clubface.

and the woods are usually numbered 1, 3, 5, and 7) and the higher the number, the steeper the loft. So you will use your 9-iron to hit the ball a shorter distance than you will hit your 5-iron; but with your 9-iron the ball should fly much higher in the air than with the 5-iron. Likewise your

1-wood (or **driver**, as it is called) will hit the ball farther (and lower) than your 5-wood.

A set of irons usually has two additional clubs with more loft (steeper angle) than the 9-iron. The iron with a little more loft than a 9-iron is the **pitching wedge**. It usually has the letter "P" on the sole. Typically the club with the most loft in a set of irons is the **sand wedge**. The sand wedge is

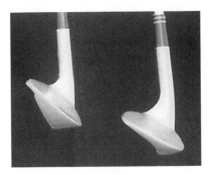

used to hit shots out of bunkers, because it has a much bigger sole that makes it easier to hit through the sand and help lift your ball out.

flat
Notice how steep the angle is on the SW (right) compared to the PW (left).

The Putter

The set of woods and irons is completed by what should be considered the most important club in the golf bag — the putter. The function of the putter is to help roll the golf ball accurately into the hole on the green. Once again, there are thousands of styles and designs from which to choose, and the one you pick should be fitted to you and be comfortable for you to use.

The putter has a grip, a shaft, a flat surface or sole on the bottom of the putter head, a toe and heel on the face, and a sweet spot in the center of the face, just like the woods and irons. The face of the putter has very little loft since it is designed to roll the ball straight across the green. The top of the putter head might be plain in design or may have a line or

lines to help identify the sweet spot or help with lining up your putt to the hole.

Four putters of different styles.

Tees

Tees are small pegs used only on the teeing ground to support the golf ball above the ground. They help the golfer keep the ball at a consistent height when teeing off. Tees are not mandatory, but they make the ball sit up so the golfer has a better chance of striking the ball cleanly.

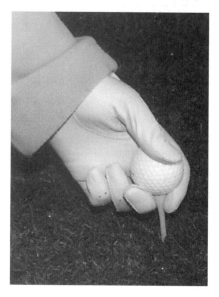

Keep plenty of tees handy during your round of golf.

Golf Glove

A golf glove is made of very thin, fine leather or synthetic material and helps increase the tackiness of the handle so it is easier to grasp with less tension. It also helps prevent blisters on your hand when you've

32

been playing golf all day or practicing for a long time. The glove should fit snugly, so with an open palm, the glove material is smooth. A glove is not mandatory when playing golf; however, it is recommended.

Right-handed golfers wear their glove on their left hand and left-handed golfers wear their glove on their right hand.

A golf glove allows for a more comfortable grip.

Golf Shoes

Golfers spend a lot of time walking. The average golf course spans about 6500 yards — that's over three miles! So the first rule about golf shoes is they should be comfortable.

When swinging a golf club you are exerting a lot of energy in a twisting motion, so most golf shoes have spikes on the bottom to help prevent slipping while swinging the club. The spikes also help to prevent slipping while walking on the course where it may be wet.

Golf shoes with spikes are not mandatory and most courses will let you play in regular athletic shoes. But if you wear shoes with spikes, be sure you don't twist your feet around or scuff your feet along while walking on the green — that grass is very delicate and can be easily damaged by spikes.

Accessories

There are lots of other accessories you may want to consider as you begin to play more golf. Most of them will not help you to be a better golfer, but they may help make the game enjoyable in other ways. So, before you play, check to see if you are prepared with such things as: a golf umbrella and other rain gear, a hat, sunglasses, a pull cart, and a travel bag (if you are taking your clubs on vacation).

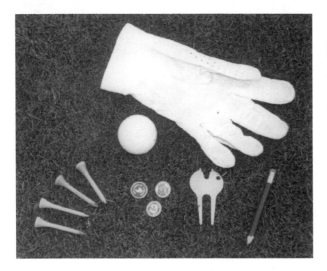

Which of these golf accessories will most likely help your game? You got it: the eraser!

Two other accessories, the **ball marker** and the **ball mark repair tool** will be introduced and discussed in the chapter on golf etiquette.

4

Swing the Club – Hit the Target

Golf is a game in which we try to safely maneuver around trees, over lakes, past hazards and other obstacles to sink the golf ball into the hole at the bottom of the flagstick — in the fewest number of strokes possible. In order to get your ball past all of the hazards and onto the green, you will have to be able to identify a good target and then hit your ball accurately to that target.

Sometimes the target you are aiming at is the center of the green; sometimes it is an open area in the fairway that will give you the best look at the green for your next shot. But in any event, in golf it is important to be able to hit the ball where you want to hit it.

(Note: Swing and set-up instructions assume a right-handed golfer.)

Let's Start With a Little Game

Here is a game you can play to see what hitting the target is like: Build a little pyramid of four golf balls with three on the bottom and one on top — that is your target. (You can practice this in your backyard — if you have enough space to do it safely — or at the practice chipping green at the golf course. For this game you can use real golf balls or plastic golf balls.)

Golf is a game of hitting targets. See if you can hit this one.

Walk about ten feet back from the target and place a golf ball on a tee in the ground. Now, using a 7-iron take ten shots at the target and see how many times you can knock it down. To hit the ball that far you don't need to swing very hard — especially if you are inside the house! Just bring the clubhead back about one to two feet and swing through about the same.

(By the way, it might be easier to play the game if you have ten golf balls, rather than chasing one golf ball around the yard ten times!)

It looks easy to hit the target, but it's not! If you hit the target ten times in a row go immediately to the telephone to call the PGA and join the tour! If not, let's see if we can help you build a golf swing that will get you closer to hitting your target more consistently.

Building a Good Golf Swing

There is more to a good golf swing (one that will give you consistency and accuracy) than getting up and hitting the ball. A good golf swing, just like constructing a house, is built on a strong foundation. In golf the foundation consists of a few fundamentals that will help you hit your target more easily.

HIT THE TARGET

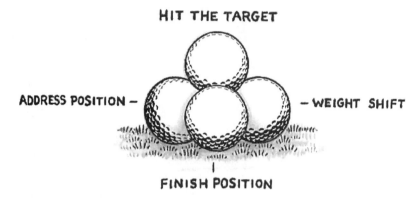

ADDRESS POSITION —   — WEIGHT SHIFT

FINISH POSITION

Learn the Building Blocks and develop a good swing.

The building blocks of a good golf swing are: learning to address the ball, learning to shift your weight as you swing, and learning to follow through to the end of the swing. If you put these building blocks into place in your swing, then no matter what kind of shot you are taking you will give yourself the best chance to swing the club and hit the target.

Building Block #1 — Address Position

When golfers talk about addressing the ball, they do not mean mailing it to the hole. (That would be easier, but it's not how you play golf!) Addressing the ball means how to line up your ball and how YOU line up TO your ball.

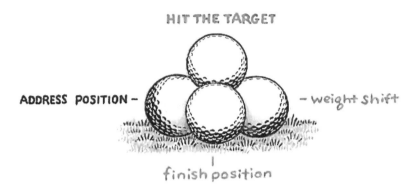

Address position includes the target line, club position, stance, and grip.

Step One: Establish a Target Line

Start by setting up your game again. Build your pyramid, walk ten feet back from the target, and place a ball on a tee in the ground.

> You can use bigger targets, too, like a pail, a cardboard box, a dinosaur, or what ever happens to be handy. If you are at the practice chipping green, you can always use the flagstick, and if you do, remember that your goal is to get close to the flagstick, not necessarily hit it.

Walk behind the ball on the tee and be sure that a straight line is formed by yourself, the ball on the tee, and the target.

Then, place a tee flat on the ground six inches in front of the ball, in line with the target and pointing to the target. In this way, you can begin to establish a **target line**, the first step to addressing the ball.

Establish a straight line to your target.

Step Two:
Club Position

Point the sweet spot right at your target.

Start with a 7-iron and set the face of the club at a 90-degree angle or "square" to the target line. The sole of the club should sit flat on the ground and the sweet spot should be

39

facing the ball and your target. (If the sole of the club is flat on the ground, the grip of the club should come up to you in such a way that your arms are hanging and relaxed in front of you.)

Take ten more nice, easy shots at the pyramid, but swing the club along the target line you have established. See how many times you hit the target using the target line.

Even if you still haven't hit the target, you are probably getting closer by using the target line.

Step Three: Stance and Posture

Notice that the target line is being used as a reference line to keep the clubface square (at 90 degrees) to the target. The rest of the address position will also be designed with reference to the target line. The next step is the **stance** or how your feet are placed. Stand so that your toes are facing the target line and with your left heel about two inches to the left of the clubhead. Your feet should be about shoulder-width apart and your knees should be slightly bent.

Line up your body to the target line too.

The body position, or **posture,** at address should be balanced with equal weight under each foot. Now rock forward toward your toes until you feel about 60 percent of your weight on the balls of your feet.

Practice the stance and posture position until you feel you are in a good, balanced position. Relax and take ten more shots at the target, still swinging the club along the target line.

Getting closer, aren't you?!

Step Four: The Grip

How you hold the club is a very important part of hitting the target. When you squeeze your hands together, can you feel the muscles in your arms and your shoulders and your back tighten up too? That is because all of those muscles are connected.

When you hold the golf club, if you squeeze your hands too tightly on the club, your whole body will tighten up and you won't be able to swing the club smoothly. That's an important point to remember as you learn the grip.

The View From Above

For the proper grip position, start by cradling the club in your hands with the grip resting across your fingers. Then wrap your fingers around the handle so your thumbs make a fairly straight line as you look down the handle of the club.

Rotate the right hand so the thumb and index finger saddle the top of the handle. Slightly pinch these two fingers together so the first joint of the thumb and the knuckle of the index finger almost touch.

The club rests along your fingers.

A relaxed grip will help you swing more smoothly.

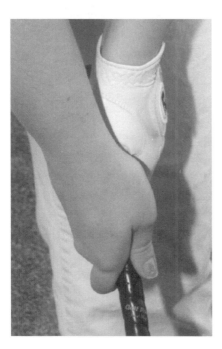

Pinch the thumb to the first knuckle on your index finger.

The View From Below

Overlap the little finger of the right hand gently over the index finger of the left hand. This is called an **overlapping grip**.

If you are having difficulty with this, then you can leave all ten fingers on the grip until you get used to holding the club. This is called a **ten-fingered grip**.

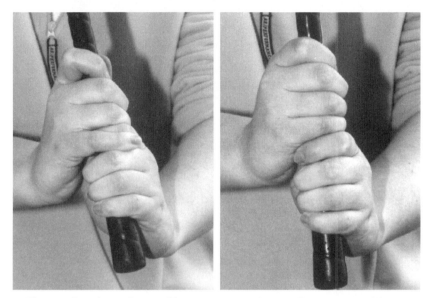

The overlapping grip provides a stable but flexible hold on the club.

The ten-finger grip is like the baseball grip.

On a scale of one to ten (with ten being as tight as you can squeeze the handle, and one feeling as though you might lose the golf club), hold the handle at about six. Avoid extreme stiffness in the arms and wrists. Keep them loose so the club swings easily and naturally. Elbows should be comfortably relaxed but extended slightly to the side of your rib cage.

Now, using that grip pressure of six, and remembering all of the things we covered in Building Block #1, step up to the target line and hit ten more balls at your target. You should be getting pretty good at coming close to the target now.

Let's review. Did you hit the target? If not, watch the clubhead travel over the tee six inches in the front of the ball. If the club travels to the left of the tee, the ball will go left of the

43

target. If the club travels to the right of the tee, the ball will travel to the right of the target. Now watch the ball travel over the tee. If both the ball and the club travel over the tee in the front, the ball will go toward the target.

The better you get at swinging the *club* over the tee on your target line, the easier it is to hit the *ball* to the target. Keep practicing! You will continue to improve and soon you will come very close to hitting the target on a regular basis — and then hitting the target a lot!

Building Block #2 — Weight Shift

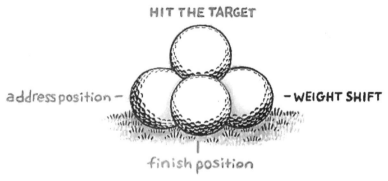

Shifting your weight lets you swing to the target.

So far we have been practicing by taking a short swing to hit the ball a short distance. To put the next building block in place, you will want to go to the full swing area of the practice range and pick a target thirty or forty yards away. Flags or other targets will probably already be set up out in the hitting area. (Be sure you are in a place where you can swing freely without hitting anyone else or without being hit by anyone else.)

Tee up the ball in your spot at the driving range. Establish your target line by standing behind the ball in line with the target. Mark your target line with a tee six inches in front of your ball, and then take your address position. Hit a few balls with your short swing so you can follow the sweet spot of the club and the ball over the mark or tee in front of the ball.

<u>Step One</u>: The Path of Your Swing

So far you have been aiming the clubface and swinging the clubhead along a fairly straight line toward the target. When you use a bigger swing, however, you will want the clubhead to trace a more circular path.

Address is evenly balanced and comfortable.

Take the clubhead back to a point where the shaft of the club is a little past parallel to the ground. Now swing the club forward to a place where the shaft is a little past parallel to the ground in front of you. Now do that several times at a slow, even pace, and have the clubhead trace a circle around you (not a straight line back and forth). The clubhead should still go out over the tee or mark that is marking your target line.

A little past parallel
for a half swing.

Trace a circular path as you
swing forward.

When you swing the club away from the ball to your right it is called the **backswing**. And when you swing the club to the ball it is called the **forward swing**.

As you swing the club back and forth, can you feel your weight shift from your back foot to your front foot? That's good. When you throw a baseball you shift your weight from your back foot to your front foot toward your target. In the golf swing you want to do the same thing. Since we want to hit the target, we also want to move toward the target!

Go through your routine for establishing the target line, club and ball position, stance and posture, and grip. Look at the sweet spot of the club, the ball and tee in front of the ball, take the club about two feet back and three feet forward, and hit the ball over the tee using the sweet spot of the club. Feel your weight move through the ball, along the target line as you make contact with the ball.

The clubhead should travel in a circular path in relation to the target line. Be very careful to swing easy and make sure no one is close to you or on the other side of the target in case you miss hit the ball.

At this point, take a few easy, half swings from your address position without hitting a ball to the target so you can think more about your technique. You can take practice swings in your backyard or in the park or almost anywhere as long as no one is near you while you are swinging. As you are taking your practice swings, concentrate on feeling the weight transfer from your back foot to your front foot.

Now, establish your target line and address position again and see if you can hit the target by using that little shift in your weight from back to front. Try this with at least twenty balls. You should gradually get very close to the target!

<u>Step Two</u>: Learn to Turn

The second part of the swing motion is the turn. The turn will be at each end of the weight transfer and will help you complete the circular path you have been drawing with the clubhead. So, on the backswing, as you move your weight to your right foot, turn slightly onto your right leg. On the forward swing, as you transfer weight to the left foot, turn slightly onto your left leg.

The motion should not be contorted in any way and, in fact, the entire golf swing should not go outside of any normal range of motion for the average golfer.

Turn onto your right leg, but you don't need to sway back.

Again, take some practice swings so you can learn to incorporate establishing your target line, the address position, the weight transfer and, finally, the turn. Then hit at least twenty golf balls, taking some practice swings between shots. As you practice you will get closer to the target.

Building Block #3 — The Finish Position

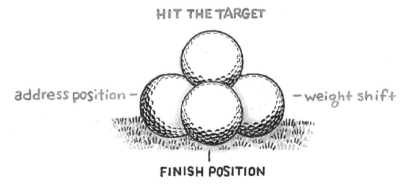

Ending at a good solid finish position will keep you in balance.

The third building block that you will use to support your goal of hitting the target is developing the proper **finish position** at the end of the golf swing.

Up to this point we have practiced with a short swing and a half swing, but on most golf shots you will hit the ball with a full golf swing. The full golf swing simply takes all of the pieces we have put together so far and adds two more pieces, the top of the backswing and the finish position.

On a full swing you will take the clubhead back farther than you did on the half swing. Still using the circular motion and the turn, take the clubhead back over the right shoulder so the end of the grip is pointing away from the target. After completing your turn, you are at the top of the backswing.

On the **follow through**, which is from **impact** to finish, put into place the building blocks discussed earlier, swing through the target line, shift your weight to the front foot, and complete the circular path to face the target. The momentum of your swing will carry the clubhead all the way to behind your head. Your weight shift should carry you to where most of your weight is on your front foot.

Turn to face your target, just like you would when throwing a ball.

Let's look at the footwork at the finish position. The left or front foot is flat on the ground and evenly balanced. The right foot is vertical to the ground with the laces facing the target and the tip of the shoe resting on the ground. You should feel as if all your weight is over your left foot.

Let's look at the body at the finish position. The legs are relaxed and slightly bent. The hips and shoulders are level and facing the target. Arms are bent at the elbows as the momentum of the clubhead carries you to your finish.

Get into a good habit of holding your finish position to the count of three, as if someone is taking your picture. This gives you a chance to evaluate how well you moved and finished to the target and how well you stayed balanced and completed your finish. Make corrections at this time so when you make another swing, it will be easier to go to the same finish position. Smile! 1-2-3 click.

> A good drill to help you find a solid finish position is to stand facing the ball and lift the golf club over your left shoulder about ear height until the end of the handle is facing the same direction you are facing. Now turn to the target and set up the proper footwork. Practice that over and over until you feel exactly where you are supposed to end up and it feels quite natural.

The importance of evaluating your finish position is that it will become a reference point for a consistent shot. Just before you start your swing, think about your finish position and soon you will be more able to repeat the same motion along the same path to the same finish.

An Important Point to Remember: Tempo

Tempo means how fast or how slow the golf swing is moving. For example in music, a fast song has a quick tempo and you might feel more energetic. A slow song has a more relaxed tempo, like a lullaby, and you might feel like taking a nap under a tree.

In the golf swing, it is better to start with a fairly slow and easy tempo, especially when the swing is very new to you. Count to four as you take your backswing. When you change direction at the top of the backswing, count to four again, with the finish being at four. As you get comfortable with the swing, the tempo will gradually become more like being on the swing at the park.

A Final Thought on the Golf Swing

All golfers, even professional players, hit a mixture of good and bad shots. Don't give up, even if it takes a while to get it right — you have a lifetime to learn it and to enjoy it!

Note to kids and parents: The GolfBook for Kids is designed to give you an introduction to the game of golf. This section on technique is a basic overview of how the golf swing works. It is important that you see a good teaching professional to make sure you are correctly executing proper technique.

Here's a golf joke for you:

Q.   What is the difference between a golfer and a skydiver?

A.   A golfer goes "whap" and then says, "Oh no!" A skydiver says, "Oh no!" and then goes "whap."

Chapter 5

Golf — Three Games in One

Golf can be viewed as a combination of three games in one: the long game, the short game, and the putting game. The long game requires a combination of power and control, the short game requires good judgment of distances and the ability to select the right club, and the putting game requires a very sensitive touch and the ability to see which way the ball will roll over the ups and downs of the green.

A golfer who is an excellent putter, but who always hits the ball into the rough from the tee, will never score well at golf and will probably find the game frustrating. Likewise with someone who can hit monster drives off the tee, but who can't putt.

Each of these three games requires a different set of skills, and to be successful at golf you really need to understand and master all three of the games at the same time. Let's look at the three games within the game of golf and see how to get the most benefit out of each by taking the least number of strokes.

The Long Game

Distance. What do golfers want more than distance? More distance! But the skill you need to master in the long game of golf is keeping your shot under control while hitting the ball a long way — a tricky balancing act. Of the two, control is certainly the more important. When your swing is under control, it is better balanced. When you master balance and control, the distance will come.

The long game clubs are the driver, the fairway woods, and the long irons. The driver is used when your longest distance is needed, usually on the tee. However, if you have not yet mastered hitting a driver with control into the fairway, a 3-wood or 5-wood would be a very good choice.

Hitting out of the fairway often calls for shots with fairway woods or long irons. If you are in the rough, choose a club with a little more loft, like a 5-wood or 7-wood. Sometimes the smart choice is to just take a 7-iron and hit the ball back out into the center of the fairway.

Another important part of the long game is planning your shot, known in golf as **course management**. Many times when you hit a long shot, you need to hit over some trouble areas (like bunkers or lakes). Sometimes the smart thing to do is to **lay up** to the trouble by hitting a shorter shot that will roll up near it without trying to go over it. Then on your next shot you can easily hit over the trouble with another shorter shot.

Remember what you learned in the last chapter — golf is a game of hitting targets. So choose a target that you know you can hit and then use the good, solid golf swing you have built to hit it! In golf that is called "using your brain." (That's a very technical term that you will come to understand better as you play more golf.)

The Short Game

For younger, newer golfers, let's consider the short game to be anywhere within about 30 yards of the flagstick or of your chosen target. This will include shots from the fairway, from bunkers near the green, from the rough around the green, and from the **apron** or closely mown area surrounding the green.

Of course, every shot in golf is designed to get you closer to your goal of getting the ball into the hole, but it's in the short game shots that you see it most clearly. If you can get the ball pretty close to the flagstick with your short game shots, you will make your task of putting a lot easier and save yourself a lot of strokes.

There are three categories of short game shots that we will cover: the **chip shot**, the **pitch shot**, and the **bunker shot.**

The Chip Shot

The chip shot is a short shot, usually near the green, in which you want to jump the ball approximately one-third of the way to the target and have it roll the other two-thirds of the way. You can use your 7-, 8-, or 9-iron for this shot depending on how fast and how far you want the ball to go.

The chip shot is considered an accuracy shot because, if you get really good at it, you may be able to get it right into the hole from around the green.

The address position and the club and ball positions should be just like you practiced with Building Block #1, except you can rotate your hands outward just a little, so that your hands are closer to the side of the grip. Establish your target line by picking a spot in front of the ball in line to the flagstick or target.

Address should be comfortable and aligned to the target.

The chip shot is a very short shot in distance to the target and requires only a very small swing, just like when you were first learning to hit the pyramid of balls. You may find you need only to take the club away about two feet or less on the backswing and follow through about three feet or so.

Use the same weight transfer and circular turn you used in the short swing. Turn to a balanced finish position, facing the target with shoulders fairly level and hands and arms moving to the target.

Your club should pass above the spot you have marked on your target line.

Use the tempo you practiced earlier. Start out smoothly at the **take away**, let the club seem as though it is pausing when changing direction at the backswing, and allow the club to swing to the balanced finish. If you find this shot difficult at first, put the ball on a tee and practice the same technique. When you start to make some good shots, then try the technique on the grass.

Pitch Shots

The pitch shot can be used for the same distance or longer than the chip shot, but flies higher. Where the chip shot flew one-third of the way to the target, the pitch shot flies about halfway or more and rolls the rest of the way.

The pitch shot can be used to hit up onto a green from the fairway, over bunkers near the green, or when you want to hit over the rough around the green. Use a pitching wedge or 9-iron for this shot.

Your address position and your swing mechanics should be the same as for the half swing discussed in Chapter 4. Apply what you know from Building Blocks #1 and #2, and bring the clubhead back about halfway for a pitch shot and follow through toward the target using your weight transfer and circular turn.

The tempo of the pitch shot is very similar to the chip shot swing. The difference is that, since the pitch shot swing is larger, you want to take a little more time to complete the swing.

Bunker Shots

There are bunkers along the fairways and there are bunkers in the fairway and there are bunkers along some sides of the greens and sometimes there are bunkers on every side of the green. Sometimes it seems like there are bunkers everywhere! In fact, some golf courses might have over a hundred bunkers!

Some bunkers are flat while others plane upward to what is called the **lip** or edge of the bunker. But whatever the size or shape of the bunker, in most instances your sand wedge will be the tool of choice to use in bunkers situated near the green.

There are actually a few differences between hitting a ball out of a bunker and the other shots you have learned. Even though there are differences, the bunker shot is still built on the same building blocks you already know.

Establish the target line just as you did before. Your target line may point straight at the flagstick, or it could aim at a target that is easier to get to, if the bunker has a high lip.

When setting up for a shot out of the bunker, you will use the same address position as you did in the earlier exercises. This time you need to wiggle your shoes down into the sand a bit so your feet won't slip during the swing.

Use the full swing you have practiced, and be sure to follow through all the way to a good finish position because the sand will have a tendency to slow your clubhead down as you swing through it. You don't need to swing harder, just swing all the way through. On your forward swing, "bounce" the clubhead against the sand behind the ball so there will be a buffer of sand between the clubface and the ball. The ball will ride out of the bunker on a blast of sand!

How to practice the bunker shot

Getting out of a bunker can be challenging, and if you don't learn how to do it right it will add a lot of strokes to your score. With a little practice, however, you can learn to do it very well.

The first rule for practicing the bunker shot is to be sure that no one is in front of you or even to the side of where you are practicing because when you are fist learning this shot the ball can scoot off your club and go flying off to the sides. You also want to be careful not to hit sand in the direction of where someone is standing —getting sand in someone's eye would be dangerous.

Don't be afraid to spray the sand out of the bunker.

If you are playing by the **Rules of Golf**, you cannot touch the sand before your shot with anything but your feet — that means, no practice shots or testing the condition of the sand during a real game. But for purposes of practice and learning, it's a good way to get the feel of how the sand shot is different from a regular shot.

> Draw a rectangle in the sand along the target line with your finger, (Again, this is just a practice drill and not within the rules, so don't do it during the game.) Take the same swing as your practice bunker swing and see if it swipes out the rectangle and sprays sand over the front lip of the bunker. This might require several practice swings.

Now you see it...

Now you don't. (If you're looking for the ball, it's in the hole!)

Now place a ball in the middle of the rectangle. Note that there is a space of sand in front of the ball and behind the ball within the boundaries of the rectangle. This means that there will be a buffer of sand between the ball and the clubface at impact. You won't feel the impact of the ball on the clubface when you hit it, and the ball should fly high with less speed and distance than on a regular shot.

With practice, you will become comfortable with the ball flying high out of the bunker with an easy swing. When starting out, it is of primary importance just to learn to get out of the bunker and onto the green, even if the ball lands at the far end of the green from the flagstick. So don't worry about accuracy at the beginning, that will come later with practice and experience.

The Putting Game   (Glove on or off)

It is always a concern to new golfers to make good, consistent tee shots and fairway shots in order to keep up with other established players. But once you gain some confidence off the tee and in the fairway, the most important part of playing good golf and lowering your scores is putting.

In putting, you want to roll the ball as easily as possible over the well-kept, manicured grass of the green right into the hole. But since the green is usually neither flat nor level, the ball will not roll in a perfectly straight line to the hole. As it rolls across slope of little hills, the ball will curve with the contour of the green. As it travels up and down these hills it will lose or gain speed. So you will need to learn how to read the green to determine which way the ball will roll, and how fast it will roll, before you hit it.

Your eyes will learn to see what is called **the break** or amount of influence from the slope of the putting surface, which curves the journey of the ball to the right or left. If you practice hard, you could develop the accuracy of a billiards champion and the **touch** and coordinated feel of a tour player.

Through practice and good technique, the golf ball will roll smoothly over the sides of the mounds and the ups and downs of the putting surface. Think of the excitement as it falls right into the hole to the sounds of your cheering friends and family!

To get ready to putt, you will once again establish your target line (remember that if the green is going to make your ball curve then your target line goes along the curve, not straight to the hole). Even though putting looks very different than a full swing, the more you can use what you already know, the more consistent all parts of your game will become.

Set the putter behind the ball and square the face to the target line. Make sure the putter rests with the sole under the sweet spot flat on the ground. Take the same grip as the chip

The grip on the putter can be a little more open than with the full swing shots.

shot, rotating your hands outward just a little, so that your hands are closer to the side of the grip. Relax so you are in an evenly balanced position and not leaning to the right or left.

Keep the grip pressure light and allow the putter to feel like it is swinging. Bring the putter back a short distance and follow through twice as far forward past the ball as you brought the club back on the backswing. For short putts, of about two feet, the putter only needs about a 3-inch backswing and should follow through about six inches after impact.

Don't think of putting as "hitting" the ball; think of putting as "rolling" the ball.

How to Practice Putting

Begin by finding a flat surface on the practice putting green. Take a small step about two feet from the hole and place a ball on the putting surface. Just like the "swing the club, hit the target" game, place a ball marker six inches in front of the ball and in line with the hole. Be sure to stand behind the ball in order to accurately line up the ball, the marker, and the hole.

Once again, establish your target line; use a marker in practice.

Circle Drill: Place five golf balls around the hole, each at a foot from the hole, and see how many you can **hole out**. Keep a score pad and pencil in your back pocket and write down at one foot, how many out of five you made. Try five more from one foot and see if your score improved. If you made eight out of ten then you made 80 percent of your putts at one foot. Very Good!

Practice the circle drill from different distances.

Now place five golf ball around the hole each at two feet and repeat the same procedure. Then do the same at three feet and so on. Challenge yourself to see if you can hole out as many putts at six feet as you did at two feet.

Here's another golf joke:

Q.   What's the easiest stroke in golf?

A.   The fourth putt!

<u>Practice, Practice, Practice</u>

Golf is like any other sport or hobby you enjoy. It's a lot of fun to play, but to get really good at it, you will have to spend some time practicing. The good news is that to practice golf you don't have to actually go out and play on a golf course. You can practice chipping in your <u>back yard</u>, you can practice driving and pitching at the driving range and you can even practice putting in your bedroom. (Please, just don't get confused and practice driving in your bedroom!)

As you perfect your technique you will gain more confidence and have more and more fun playing golf. If you have a short, par-3 course or "pitch and putt" course where you live, you can begin to practice your shots there, and when you have improved enough, you can graduate to a regulation golf course.

Some Rules to Know

In *The GolfBook for Kids* we won't cover all the rules of golf. What's most important for beginning players to learn is how to swing the club properly, how to chip, how to putt, and to enjoy the game.

To understand how the game works, however, you need to know the basic rules, so we'll cover the most important ones. Then, as your skill level improves, you will be able to incorporate more of the rules into your play.

The Official Rules of Golf are written and administered jointly by the United States Golf Association and The Royal & Ancient Golf Club of St. Andrews, Scotland. These rules govern any competitive golf match or any round that will be used to calculate your **handicap** (which is covered in more detail at the end of the chapter).

☆ Whose Turn Is It, Anyway?

At the first hole the order of play is decided randomly. Very often what golfers do is stand in a circle and toss a tee into the air; the player to whom it's pointing when it lands goes first. Toss it again to see who goes second, third, and fourth.

Flip a tee to see who goes first.

Throughout the rest of the hole, the one who is the farthest away from the hole hits first. This way the entire group stays close together, instead of one person getting way ahead, which can be distracting and dangerous. Everyone stays behind the person hitting. After the hit, everyone moves up toward the next ball to be hit. That way no one gets hit by a shot coming up from behind. Because getting hit by a ball or a club could cause serious injury, safety is very important in golf.

When you finish the hole and you go to the next tee, the one with the best score on the previous hole goes first. That is called having the **honor.** The one with the second best score goes next and so on. After you've hit your tee shots, the order of play is, once again, determined by who is farthest from the hole until you are finished with that hole.

After play is completed on each hole and your group has moved to the next tee, mark the scores for each player on the **score card**.

✦ Keeping Score

Keeping score in golf, for the most part, is pretty simple — each swing counts as a stroke. Even if you attempt to hit the ball but miss (a **whiff**), it counts as a stroke. Add up all your strokes to get your total for the hole. Add up the total for all of the holes to get your total for the entire round.

Every golf course provides golfers with a score card so players can keep score for their round of golf. The score card usually includes lots of valuable information to golfers about the course. For instance, the score card will tell you the distance for each hole from the forward, middle, and back tees and the total distance of the course.

The score card has lots of valuable information for golfers.

Score cards will sometimes provide a map to show which direction the hole goes, in case it is not evident from simply looking down the fairway. If the hole is a dogleg and you cannot see around the corner, the diagram on the score card may show you where any bunkers or water hazards are located. Knowing that information is pretty handy if you are playing a course for the first time!

If a golf course has certain **local rules** that you need to know about as you play, they will provide that information on the score card as well. Local rules are rules that apply only to that course and are not covered in the general Rules of Golf. For example, if a golf course has high tension wires running above a fairway, a local rule would describe what to do if your ball is deflected by the wire.

Other information that is generally provided on the score card is:

Slope rating — a rating system for comparing golf courses to one another in degree of difficulty (a course with a slope of 125 would be more difficult than one with a slope of 118)

Course rating — a rating system that compares golf courses by yardage and degree of difficulty according to the score a **scratch golfer** would get on the course (a course with a rating of 74.1 would be more difficult than a course with a rating of 71.5).

Handicap rating for each hole — a rating system for comparing the holes on the course for degree of difficulty (the #1 handicap hole is the most difficult on the course and the #18 is the easiest).

Parent's Note: The GolfBook for Kids is written for a rather wide age range of golfers (five years old to thirteen years old). Obviously, the range of abilities in those ages will also vary greatly. For the younger players, it's probably a good idea to forget about keeping score until later. Concentrate on learning to swing the club, to get the ball onto the green, and to putt.

Penalty Strokes

The simple part of keeping score in golf is counting the times you actually swing at the ball; sometimes, however, you may have to add penalty strokes if you get into trouble. Here are a couple of the main penalty strokes you need to know about:

Out of Bounds — The White Stakes

If you hit the ball out of bounds, and you are sure that it is out of bounds, you need to hit a second ball. The penalty for out of bounds is called **stroke and distance**. If you hit your tee shot and it went out of bounds, you would count that as one stroke. You would tee up another ball, that ball now **lies** two as it sits on the tee. And when you hit that ball it then lies three wherever it lands.

Water Hazards — Yellow Stakes and Red Stakes

Sometimes when your ball lands in a water hazard you will actually be able to hit it. If that is the case, by all means go ahead, and there is no penalty. But if your ball is not playable out of the hazard, you must take a one stroke penalty and

drop a ball back into play. But, depending on whether you are in a water hazard or a lateral water hazard, there are a few options on where you may drop the ball.

Here are the options:

From a water hazard (yellow stakes or lines) —

1) Play a ball from as near as possible to the place where the original ball was played.

2) Drop a ball behind the water hazard, keeping the point where the original ball crossed into the hazard, directly between the hole and where the ball is dropped. (You can go as far back behind the hazard as you like, as long as you make a straight line using the hole, the point where your ball went into the hazard, and where the ball is dropped.)

From a lateral water hazard (red stakes or lines) —

You can use options 1 or 2 above, or

3) Drop a ball next to the hazard (on either side), within two club lengths from the exact point where the ball entered the hazard, but no nearer the hole.

Bunkers

There is no penalty for landing in the bunker, just the challenge of getting your ball out again. However, when you address the ball in the bunker you may not touch the head of the club in the sand. If your club does touch the sand before your forward swing, there is a two-stroke penalty!

Unplayable Lies

Your ball will sometimes come to rest in a place where you just can't hit it. Perhaps your ball is sitting right up against the base of a tree, or landed in the branch of a tree and didn't come down, or is stuck in the middle of a blackberry patch. In any event, the ball is somewhere where you can't hit it. That is called an **unplayable lie**.

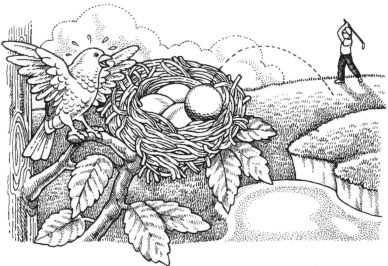

The unplayable lie can be very upsetting — even for the golfer!

If you find yourself with an unplayable lie, you must drop the ball (or another ball, if you can identify your ball but can't get it) in a spot from which you can hit it and count a one stroke penalty.

Your options are similar to the lateral water hazard:

1) Play a ball from as near as possible to the place where the original ball was played.

2) Drop a ball behind the point where the original ball lies, keeping the point where the original ball was, directly between the hole and where the ball is dropped. (You can go as far back as you like behind the point where your ball was, as long as you make a straight line using the hole, the point where your ball was, and where the ball is dropped.)

3) Drop a ball within two club lengths of the place where the ball lies, but no nearer the hole.

Lost Golf Ball

A **lost ball** during a round of golf is not a happy event. It's sad because the ball cost you some money; what's even sadder, though, is it will also cost you a stroke. If you lose a golf ball during a round (and it's not in a water hazard or out of bounds), you must hit another ball from the place where you hit the original shot and count a one-stroke penalty.

But, what if you are not sure the ball is lost?

If you just hit your ball and it seems like it may be lost (for instance, you hit the ball into some dense trees or long grass, and those areas are in bounds) you should announce you are hitting a **provisional ball**. A provisional ball is a ball hit from the same spot where your original ball was hit, that will be played again "provided" you do not find the original ball.

Hitting a provisional ball helps save time so the golfer does not have to walk all the way back to where the original shot was hit, once it is discovered for certain the original ball is lost. You have up to five minutes to locate your original ball, and then it is officially a lost ball. You must then play your provisional (remember the provisional ball lies three because of the one stroke penalty).

If you find the original ball you must play that one according to whatever rule applies (if it's playable you can hit it; if it's unplayable, use the rule for an unplayable lie, etc.). If you happen to find just any ball, you may not assume it is yours. You must be able to actually identify your ball before you can play it as your own.

You can play your provisional ball up to the place where your original ball is likely to be. After that if you play the provisional, the original ball is deemed to be lost and you must continue to play the provisional ball (adding the penalty stroke). If you play the provisional ball after you have actually found the original ball (and the original is in bounds and not in a water hazard), you also have a two-stroke penalty for playing a **wrong ball.**

Yikes! The best thing to do is be careful not to lose a ball!

Relief Situations

Here are three examples of situations in which you can move your ball without a penalty:

1) If your ball lands on or next to an artificial obstruction, such as a cart path or a water fountain, that prohibits or blocks your swing or your ability to hit the ball;

Mark the spot where your ball lies by placing a tee on the ground by the ball.

This spot is not the closest spot to the original lie.

This lie is closer to the original lie. It is the proper place to drop — no nearer the hole.

2) If your ball lands in an area marked "Ground Under Repair," which is an area that is under construction by the golf course's greens crew;

3) If your ball lands in **casual water**, which is a temporary accumulation of water on the golf course.

You may remove your ball from casual water and drop it with no penalty — within one club length, no nearer the hole.

Otherwise you must follow the most famous of all the rules of golf: Play it as it lies.

Dropping a Ball

In a situation where you have the option to drop a ball, such as when your ball has landed on a cart path or in a hazard, the procedure for dropping it is simple: You select a spot that is legal for a drop (i.e., next to the cart path, or away

from the water sprin-
kler), stand erect with
your arm straight out at
shoulder height, and
drop the ball.

You must drop the
ball within one club
length of the desig-
nated legal spot, and no
closer to the hole.

*If the ball rolls back
onto the cart path
you may drop it again.*

Competitive Play

As you become better at the game of golf you may be interested in playing golf in some tournaments in your area or
having a competition with a friend. This can be a great way to
improve your game and to play with golfers of different levels
of ability.

There are two main styles of play in competitive golf: **match
play** and **stroke play**. In match play the winner is determined
by which player has won the greatest number of holes in the
contest. A hole is won by the player with the fewest strokes.
In stroke play the winner is the one who completes the entire
round in the fewest total number of strokes.

Since the two styles focus on such different aspects of the game, the strategies for success in the styles are very different. In match play, because you are trying to win as many holes as possible, you may employ a riskier strategy, knowing that if you get into trouble you have the opportunity to make it up on the next hole, since your strokes don't accumulate against you. In stroke play, because your total strokes do accumulate against you, you may want to be more careful in your strategy, since any mistake you make will carry with you through the entire round.

Handicap

Like competitors in many other sports, golfers can use a handicap system to allow competitors of different abilities to play a match together. A handicap is determined through a somewhat complex system of calculation depending on the recent scores you have submitted and the difficulty of the courses played. A golf handicap can be calculated by your local golf course or some golf shops, but to be used in a USGA-sanctioned tournament, a handicap must be done by a USGA authorized system.

Using the handicap system, players of different skill levels can compete with each other in a golf tournament by having the lower-handicap player give strokes to the higher-handicap player to balance out their average scores. For instance, if a 10-handicap player is playing against an 18-handicap player, the 10-handicap player would give the 18-handicap player 8 strokes. (In golf, the lower the handicap number, the better the player averages in a round of golf.)

The 10-handicap player would provide a one-stroke advantage to the 18-handicap player on each of the eight hardest holes on the course, as determined by the handicap rating for each hole, described above. The one who plays the best as compared to their typical game will win the event.

Summary

The Rules of Golf can sometimes be a bit hard to figure out — even for lifelong golfers! They were certainly not designed to make the game easier. But these are the rules that govern play for the entire world of golfers from the best pro on the tour to the local junior tournament in your town. So it's a good idea to become familiar with how they work.

As your game improves and you begin to play more and more, you will probably want to spend some time getting to know the full set of rules. And, of course, if you ever have trouble sleeping at night, the Rules of Golf will make a great bedside companion!

Golf Etiquette — How to Win Friends and Influence Golfers!

Golf etiquette is an extremely important part of the game of golf. The etiquette golfers show to one another out on the course is one of the things that distinguishes golf from all other sports. But what is etiquette?

Etiquette has to do with manners. It is the courtesy we show to other people and how we communicate our respect for them and how we show them how important we think they are. Whether we are talking about etiquette at the dinner table, in school, in our family or out at the movies with our friends, etiquette is important.

In golf, etiquette concerns the courtesies that golfers extend to one another on the course to make the game safe and enjoyable. The rules of etiquette enable golfers to concentrate on playing their game without being interrupted by loud noises, long delays or damage to the course.

Golf is a game that requires a lot of concentration. If you are trying to make a putt, or hit your tee shot into a narrow fairway, it will be more difficult to focus your attention if someone is running around the tee, or even talking loudly.

A few rules of etiquette apply in all situations on the golf course and the practice range;   other rules of etiquette are particular to certain circumstances, especially on the green. Let's cover the general applications of golf etiquette and then discuss in detail some of the specific things that every good golfer needs to know.

General Golf Etiquette Rules

Safety

The first and foremost rule of golf and golf etiquette is safety. Without some good common sense, and a notion of how hard golf balls and clubs are, golfers will find that a golf course can be a very dangerous place. So here are some safety rules to always follow on the golf course:

When you take a practice swing, be sure you are not facing or swinging toward another person (rocks and sticks and grass can fly up and hit them in the eye.)

To quote Abraham Lincoln, golf is a game that should be played,
"with mallets toward none."

Be aware of when other people are hitting or practicing their swing so you don't walk around them — and don't swing your clubs when someone is walking around you.

> Every year scores of young golfers get whacked on the noggin with titanium golf clubs — OUCH!! Never swing your clubs unless you are SURE there is no one near you!

If you hit a ball and it looks like it is going toward another golfer, holler "**Fore**!" as loudly as you can so they can get out of the way. This is the one time on a golf course when you are allowed to yell, so don't be shy about it.

After you hit your tee shot, wait until everyone in your group has hit before you take even one step down the fairway toward your ball.

In the fairway, don't get ahead of others in your group; their shots could go off line and hit you.

Quiet

Quiet is required on the golf course (except if you are hollering "Fore!"). Golf requires lots of concentration, and even if the people in your immediate group don't seem to be bothered by noise, remember, there are lots of other groups all around you who will be bothered.

Always walk. Running around is distracting and causes damage to the course. Walk quickly, but lightly.

Pace of Play

As more and more people begin to play golf, and the courses become more crowded, there is a risk that the game will take much longer to play. It doesn't have to take longer, though, if each golfer is careful to keep the game moving along. So here are some things you can do to maintain a good pace of play:

Take only one practice swing for each shot, then hit the ball. (Remember: If you take 120 shots in a game and you take an extra thirty seconds for each one, you will add one whole hour to the length of your golf game.)

Plan your shot before it is your turn. While you are waiting for those ahead of you to hit, decide in what direction you are going to play and which club you are going to use.

As you approach the green, determine in which direction the next tee is located and leave your clubs (or park your cart) on that side of the green.

By placing your clubs on the side of the green from which you will exit, you will save a lot of time.

Keep up with the golfers in the group ahead of you. For instance, when they finish putting and leave the green you should be ready to hit your shots to the green. You will play better golf if you are prepared and waiting for the group ahead of you than if you are hurrying to catch up.

Playing Through

If one group is playing slowly and is not keeping up with the group ahead of them, the group behind the slow group might want to pass them and move ahead. This is referred to as **playing through**.

If you want to let another group play through, the best place to do so is on the green. When all of the members of your group are on the green, mark your golf balls and stand to the side of the green. Signal to the group behind that it is safe for them to hit up and watch each of their shots approach the green, being careful to stay out of the way.

While they are walking to the green, finish your putts. Replace the flagstick and move to the next tee. After the group behind has finished putting out, you can wait for them to hit their tee shots. Then wait a few moments longer while they hit their second shots and they move beyond the range of your drives before you hit.

You may find other times in the game that are just as convenient to let a group play through. The important thing to remember is that you should be courteous about letting faster groups play through if there is a convenient time and room ahead for them to play.

The two things that will make playing through easy and agreeable are safety and courtesy — the two essential components of golf etiquette!

Pull Carts

To drive a motorized cart on a golf course, you generally need a driver's license, so most readers of this book will have to wait a while for that experience. You don't need a license to use a pull cart, but some common sense would be helpful. Here are a few tips on using pull carts:

- Pull the cart around the tees, not over them.
- Pull the carts around the bunkers, not between the bunkers and the greens.
- Don't bring your carts too close to the greens. Leave your cart at least ten feet away.
- If someone else is hitting, stop rolling your cart.

On the Teeing Ground

When you are on the tee, the most important thing to keep in mind is to respect the person hitting. Any unnecessary movements or noises are not appreciated by someone who is trying to concentrate on hitting a straight shot down the fairway.

Stand away from the player who is hitting, at least far enough to be out of their peripheral vision. Use common sense to find a good place to stand. Consider safety and courtesy and be sure you are out of range of the golf club and the golf ball. That way they will be able to hit their shot without worrying about hitting you.

Stay behind the person hitting — WAY behind!

Generally the forward, middle, and back tees are somewhat close to one another; if they are, your group can hit in the order of who has the honor. It the forward tees are far ahead of the middle or back tees, then the person in your group who is hitting from the tees that are farthest back should hit first. In this way, all the golfers will be safe and the pace of your group will be improved.

Watch the shots of everyone in your group and pick a landmark that identifies where the ball went. It will save time if you can help to locate someone else's ball.

Don't shout "You Da Man!" after every shot.

Remember to be quiet — rattling through your golf bag for a club or crumpling a bag of potato chips, for instance, would be considered a distraction when someone is hitting.

In the Fairway

Etiquette in the fairway is very similar to that on the tee, except that in the fairway the players are often more spread out depending on where their shots all landed. Once again, it is important to be aware of where the other members of your group are located before you hit. You want to be sure that you are not hitting your ball near where someone is standing or looking for their ball. And you want to determine whether it is your turn, or if you should wait for someone else to go ahead of you.

If you lose a ball, give a quick look in the general area where you last saw it. If it appears as though you are going to have some difficulty finding it, drop another ball and play on. If it looks like you are going to take longer than a few minutes, and there is a group behind you, let the group behind play through. Then be sure to give them room ahead before you resume play. (Never hit your ball into the group ahead of you — that is very dangerous!)

<u>Divots</u>

In Chapter 2, when describing the fairway, we mentioned that divots will often be displaced when you hit a shot from the fairway (the same is true when you are in the rough). We also said that replacing your divot is important because by replacing them you give the grass a chance to grow back and enable the course to heal itself.

There is another important reason to replace your divots, having to do with the most well known rule of golf — play it as it lies. The Rules of Golf require golfers to play their shots from wherever they land, even if the ball lands in someone else's divot hole!

Tough break! You landed in the divot hole of a very inconsiderate golfer.

It is quite difficult to hit a solid shot if you are hitting the ball out of a divot hole. As the ball leaves the indentation in the ground, it will be deflected by the edges of the divot hole.

When you replace your divot, you are not only helping the course to heal itself and restore its natural beauty, you are doing a favor for a golfer you will probably never meet. If each member of the community of golfers chips in to keep the course in good shape, the entire community benefits. Of course, if they all chip in, no one would need to putt!

Bunkers

Landing in a bunker can be one of the most difficult experiences on the golf course; sometimes it can take several tries to get out. If that happens, remain calm and rely on the strong swing that you have built. It won't let you down!

And when the inevitable happens and your ball lands in the bunker, there are a few rules of golf etiquette you should know:

- Enter from the low side of the bunker nearest your ball. Maintaining the edges on the bunker is difficult and if they cave in it is hard to repair them.

Enter the bunker from the low side, closest to your ball. Ooops! Be careful not to ground your club.

If you enter from the high side you will break down the front wall of the bunker.

- When you are finished with your shot (or shots) from the bunker, use the rake provided by the course to smoothly rake out all evidence of your ball, your shot, and your footprints.

Rake out all traces of your shot and your footprints, the other golfers will thank you!

- Follow the course's local rules about where to leave the rake (inside or outside the bunker) when you are finished raking.

Raking bunkers is a courtesy that golfers extend to one another, because if a ball lands in someone else's footprint or the mark left by their shot, it can make an already difficult shot even tougher!

On the Green

The putting green is a very special place to golfers. You will notice that, when golfers are on the green, they walk softly, speak quietly, and are careful not to disturb the other golfers. Remember that one half of all the strokes allotted for par are putts! So golfers like to concentrate as much as they can when they are putting.

Fragile — Handle With Care

The first thing to realize when you walk onto the green is that the grass is very delicate and even your footprints can be damaging to the green. So walk softly and be careful not to damage the grass with your shoes, spikes, or equipment.

Stepping Over the Ball Path

Another thing to notice as soon as you step out onto the green is the location of everyone's ball, so you don't tread on the path another golfer's ball will follow on its way to the hole. The best route to your own ball is to walk behind any other balls lying on the green.

If you need to cross the path of a ball lying on the green, step over it so your footprint will not make any depression along the line where the golfer is going to putt.

Repair Your Ball Marks

One of the great thrills in golf is to watch your well-hit shot sail through the air, land on the green, and roll up to the flagstick. What an exciting feeling! But when the ball hits the surface of the green, it can create a mark on the green.

When your approach shot hits the green it can damage the surface.

When your ball makes a mark on the green, take out your handy-dandy ball-mark repair tool and fix it. By fixing the mark, you will be ensuring that the golfers who play behind you will have a smooth surface free from blemishes.

The ball-mark repair tool is a handy device used to quickly repair damage to the green.

The proper way to fix a ball mark is to gently pull the grass back over the top of the mark the grass that has been pushed back. Then use your tool to go around the mark and even out the edges. Finally, smooth out the mark by patting it down with your hand or by lightly stepping on it.

Pull the grass back to where it was, lift and smooth the edges.

When you're done, it should be so smooth that you would want to putt over it yourself!

If you have time while waiting for the others to putt, you may want to 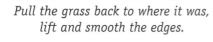 fix one or two other ball marks that less considerate golfers have failed to repair.

Marking Your Ball

When you are on the green, the Rules of Golf allow you to mark and clean your ball. By cleaning the dirt off your ball, you will ensure that you get a nice even roll when you putt; by marking it, you will ensure that you put the ball back in exactly the same spot when you are ready to putt.

Place a coin or a ball marker directly behind your golf ball, on the opposite side of the ball from the hole, then lift your ball. (Don't lift the ball first!) When you are ready to putt, place your ball back down where it was in front of the marker, then remove the marker.

While one person is marking her ball, others are lining up their putts — it helps the pace of play.

Removing/Tending the Flagstick

When a golfer is putting, the flagstick must be removed from the hole. Simply pick it straight up to avoid bashing it against the lip and damaging the edge of the hole. Take the flagstick to the side of the green and gently lay it down so the knob on the end of the flagstick is off the green.

A golfer who has a long putt may not be able to see the hole very well. In this instance, another golfer in the group can **tend the flagstick** for that golfer.

When you tend the flagstick for another golfer:

- Stand to the side of the hole, making sure your shadow does not fall over the hole or across the putting line of the golfer.

- Stand about an arm's length away from the hole, make sure you are not standing on anyone else's putting line and that you do not step on or near the hole.

- Hold the flag against the flagstick to keep it from flapping in the breeze.

- As the ball rolls toward the hole, lift the flagstick straight out, walk quietly to the side of the green, and lay it down as described above.

Shadows are on the ball path and over the hole, flag flaps in the breeze.

Shadows are away from hole, flag is held against flagstick.

General Green Etiquette

- When your group is finished putting out, carefully replace the flagstick without damaging the sides of the hole, move off the green, and proceed to the next tee.

- Mark your scores on the next tee, not on the green. This will allow the next group to begin their shots to the green as soon as you are done and benefits all the groups behind you.

  By marking scores on the next tee, not on the green, you allow the group behind to hit to the green quicker.

Good Golf Etiquette at the Practice Areas

Practice is a very important part of the game of golf — just as it's an important part of any game. Lots of people go to driving ranges and putting greens to practice their swing and putting technique.

Remember, good golf etiquette is required at the practice area as well as on the course. At the practice area, golfers are concentrating on improving and correcting their swings and that can only be done where there is a minimum of distraction. Demonstrate that you understand and appreciate good golf etiquette even when you are at the practice areas.

- Only practice sensible, controlled golf shots (risky, trick shots can be very dangerous)

- Keep voices at a low level so others won't be disturbed

- Take practice swings only in the designated areas

- Stay back from the hitting area (never go out to retrieve a ball or tee)

- Don't hit at the guy in the **ball picker**

- Aim at targets within the range (not over the fences in back or sides)

- Walk a safe distance back from other golfers' back swings

Here are two golfers who are in danger of getting hit at the driving range.

It is possible to be a great golfer without ever having a great score. The way to do it is to understand the rules of golf etiquette and to always make them a part of your game. If you do, you will never be lacking friends who would love to play a round of golf with you!

8

Bringing it all Together at the Spirit Brook Golf Club : A Short Story

Rise and Shine!

Sunlight seemed to flash through the bedroom window extra early on Saturday morning, startling Amy as she opened her eyes. A split second later she realized this was the day she both dreaded and looked forward to.

Her dad was sitting at the table and peered over his morning paper. "So, are you ready to shoot seventy-two today?" he inquired with a grin.

"Sure, Dad," she replied sarcastically, "and after that I'll play the second hole!"

Her dad chuckled and pushed her chair out for her. The welcoming aroma of her favorite breakfast, Swedish pancakes, awaited her at the table. She realized her dad had made them just for her since she was playing in her first junior golf tournament.

"Thanks, Dad," she said, reassured that he knew how she felt. At thirteen years old, she was nervous and didn't really believe her skill in golf made her ready for tournament competition.

What if I can't keep up with the good players? she thought. *What if I can't get over the water hazards?* She decided not to open that topic for discussion.

She sighed and picked up her brand-new navy-blue golf bag. She had organized and cleaned her clubs the night before and made sure she had plenty of tees and markers and her ball mark repair tool. Amy was so excited she had even shined her golf shoes!

Her dad showed her how to mark her golf balls with her own identifiable mark and Amy chose a cat with whiskers as hers. She was interested to learn it was a two-stroke penalty if she hit someone else's golf ball, so being able to clearly identify her own ball was a good idea. She marked a dozen balls and packed them into her golf bag, hoping that a dozen would be enough!

She had been taking lessons for about a year and she loved golf. Her instructor told her she was capable of playing in the tournament and to enter with the idea that it would be a great experience. "Don't worry about being terrible or expect to be fabulous," he said. "Just play golf and see if you like the extra challenge."

Amy's dad dropped her off at the pro shop in plenty of time for her to check in, stretch and loosen up, and spend a little time chipping and putting to get used to the speed of the practice green. She noticed how fast the green was at that early hour of the morning.

The First-Tee Jitters

The tournament had already begun. Amy watched as several groups teed off. She was glad she had been placed in the last foursome, even though it meant playing with Franklin, the best player in the Boy's Division. It also meant she could play with her best friend, Karen, a four-year veteran of the game. They were both in the Girl's Division, although Karen was in the Championship **flight** and Amy, as a beginner, was in the third flight.

Amy noticed Karen walking toward her, waving and smiling. Like always, she had a bounce in her step and appeared calm and happy. Amy ran over to her. "I'm so nervous! But I'm really glad we're playing together!"

"Trust me on this one," answered Karen enthusiastically. "This will be a blast!"

They noticed Franklin walking in their direction just as the starter announced their names as being on deck. They knew this meant they were next to tee off.

"Anybody nervous?" asked Franklin, peering from under his cap with a sly smile. "Where's Byron?"

"Very funny and I haven't seen him yet," Amy replied to his two questions.

The starter announced the foursome to the tee just as Byron came running up the path with his bag of clubs jangling over his shoulder. He was tall for his twelve years, a foot taller than Franklin and two years older. "I had to run home 'cause I forgot my putter and then I had to stand in line forever just to get a doughnut," he announced as he was gasping for air.

The four competitors determined the order of play by standing in a circle and tossing a tee into the air. It landed with the pointed end facing Karen, so she had the honor. They tossed the tee again to determine that Byron would tee off second, once again to see that Amy would go third, and that meant Franklin was last.

The first hole at Spirit Brook Golf Club was a fairly straight, 350-yard par 4. A beautiful old oak tree shaded the rough on the left side, but other than that, it was a good starting hole with little trouble **through the green**.

The forward and middle tees were within five yards of each other. The local **tournament rule sheet** designated Amy and Karen to play the forward tees today and Franklin and Byron to play the middle tees. The rule sheet also stated that the players should hole out all putts and they would be playing **summer rules,** not **winter rules**.

As soon as the group ahead was safely out of range, Karen teed up, aligned her shot, addressed the ball, and fired to a good finish in what seemed like only a few seconds. She made a nice smooth swing with good tempo and sent a beautiful tee shot down the middle of the fairway about 200 yards. She watched her ball land, noted its position, then picked up her tee and walked to a safe place away from the teeing ground.

Byron searched through his mixed-up bag of clubs until he found his driver. He hooked his shot into the rough and over by the oak tree on the left. Luckily, he still had a clear shot to the green, but he would be looking at it from under the spreading branches.

Amy was up next and she thought, "Here goes nothing." She decided to use her 3-wood since it was early in the round and she needed a few good swings before she'd feel comfortable with her driver. Her hands were shaking, but she managed to make a smooth, balanced swing and hit the sweet spot just right. She watched her drive draw perfectly down the left side of the fairway.

"Nice shot," complimented Franklin as he teed up. True to his reputation, Franklin smacked a terrific drive a few yards past Karen's, right down the center of the fairway. They were off and Amy thought to herself, "So far so good."

Byron was **away,** so it was his turn to hit a second shot. The ball had nestled down into the long grass of the rough, so Byron decided to hit an extra club — whereas he would have normally hit a 6-iron from that distance, he chose a 5-iron instead. The rough caught his club anyway and he missed the green to the right. He was lying two.

The green was long and narrow and Amy's approach shot had landed about five yards short of it. The **pin** was in the back and left her about twenty yards away. She thought about hitting her pitching wedge, but remembered that, in this case, the 7-iron would give her a more accurate shot.

She watched cautiously as the ball rolled toward the hole then broke to the right and rolled about twelve feet to the right of the **cup**. Amy was disappointed she hadn't read the break correctly.

When the first hole was over Amy had a bogey, Karen and Franklin had scored pars and Byron struggled in with a double-bogey 6. The foursome moved on to the 2nd tee and Amy relaxed a little, realizing she had played pretty well considering it was the first hole of her first tournament ever.

The 9th Hole – Making the Turn

The foursome moved from hole to hole, playing well, but encountering the occasional bunkers, hazards, and out of bounds stakes. Byron had settled down somewhat from his morning ordeal and was playing a little better.

The 9th hole at Spirit Brook was called, affectionately, Blues Lagoon. Water bordered the right front and side of the 135-yard, par-3 green and a treacherous jungle of shrubs guarded the left side. The only safe place to camp if you happened to miss the green was short left.

Franklin, with the best score of par on the previous par-5 hole, had the honor. He thought to himself, "...5-iron or 6-iron? The 5-iron will make it to the green, but there's a good chance I could miss it to the right. The 6-iron might be a little short but I could aim slightly to the left side and chip up for par or maybe make birdie." Franklin knew his odds of hitting this two-tiered green were not as good as he would have liked, but he knew that by thinking through his shot he would have the best chance for success.

The other three in his foursome stood back quietly while Franklin quickly lined up his shot to the left side of the green. He took his address and fired to a balanced finish position, facing his target. The ball flew high and landed softly on the front left edge of the green. He was satisfied that the 6-iron had been the right club.

"Beautiful!" exclaimed Amy. She was learning a lot just by watching the more skillful players. Karen had already chosen a 7-iron and quickly and confidently hit her shot. The ball faded slightly right and Karen held her breath as the ball headed toward the water hazard. "Straighten out," she commanded to the ball as it landed on the right side of the green just short of **pin-high**. Karen and Amy each gave a sigh of relief.

"Hey Byron, you're up," called Franklin. Byron had put his scorecard somewhere in his golf bag on the last hole and wanted to check the yardage. He thought to himself, "I could swing really hard with an 8-iron and it's the perfect distance to the flag." Byron jogged to the tee and hurriedly took a couple of practice swings.

"If you were looking for the yardage, you could have asked me," commented Franklin.

"Isn't asking advice against the rules?" inquired Byron.

"Stuff like yardage is public knowledge, so it's okay to ask. Besides, the marker is right next to you," answered Franklin, pointing to the ground and trying to be patient. He knew Byron had only been playing golf about a year.

Karen and Franklin both glanced back to see if the group behind was catching up to them. Whack! Byron hit his tee shot a little fat and the ball landed in front of the green. "Gee, I did it again," he thought to himself. "I rushed that shot."

104

Amy teed off last and she knew she would be ecstatic if she could just make it over the water hazard. Her shot landed on dry ground but it wasn't quite enough; the ball rolled back into the water. She remembered her options for yellow stakes and she pulled another ball out from her pocket. She elected to hit from the teeing ground and on her second try she made it safely onto the front center of the green, now lying three.

Franklin could see from the tee that he was away and therefore next to take a turn. He walked quickly ahead while thinking he could chip up pretty accurately with an 8-iron. It jumped and ran easily to the hole and he watched it stop about six inches past the flagstick.

"Oh! That's a **gimmie**," declared Byron. "I'd give you that if this wasn't a tournament. Go ahead and finish out."

"Thanks," answered Franklin. Since his ball wasn't in anyone's line, he easily tapped in for par. Karen, whose ball was marked closest to the hole, had carefully placed the flagstick on the side of the green and fixed Amy's ball mark, her own, and two others left behind by forgetful golfers.

Byron studied the break of his putt and was ready as soon as Franklin reached down and removed his ball from the hole with his hand. He relaxed, took a deep breath and glanced one final time at the hole. With good tempo and timing, he rolled the ball with authority up the slight incline and watched the ball break slightly right and . . . into the hole!

"ALL RIGHT!" Byron enunciated slowly. He performed a stylish strut toward the hole while being careful of his footsteps on the green.

"Wow! You sunk a forty foot putt!" declared Franklin. "What a great birdie!"

Amy putted next. She made sure she put enough speed on the ball to end up just a foot past the cup and sunk it for a double-bogey five. She considered herself fortunate.

Karen **lipped out** her birdie putt and tapped in for an easy par. Her goal for the day was to see how many greens she could hit in regulation. This made six greens so far today. She just thought to herself, "No pressure – just try to hit the center of the green or on the green anywhere and two-putt." She just might shoot her best score ever.

On the way to the 10th tee, they all picked up their bags and pulled out their scorecards as they walked. Karen looked back at the previous teeing ground and noticed the group behind just arriving. "Let's get going and not stop too long at **the turn**." she said. "I'd rather be waiting for the group ahead of us and not just trying to keep up. We'll all play better if we don't feel rushed."

Byron gave this some serious thought. Karen was calm and methodical; she seemed to never get flustered. "Maybe that's why her game was so steady and consistent," he thought to himself, "She had the poise of a tour player on the golf course."

"Did you make a five on that last hole?" Karen asked Amy. "A pretty good five for going in the water," answered Amy. Each of the four players was assigned to keep another player's score along with their own, since this was a tournament.

The **front 9** was over and after grabbing a quick drink of water, they headed for the **back 9**. Karen and Amy chatted and added up their scores for the front while they waited for the group ahead to hit and move out of range. Amy verified Karen's score of 41 and was excited to hear she had scored a 52 – her best ever! She tried not to add up her score during the round, thinking it would just make her more nervous.

The Finishing Hole

After an exciting back 9 full of pars and bogeys and a couple of double-bogeys (and a few disaster holes), the foursome now approached the 18th hole. The 18th is the #1 **handicap hole** on the course – 460 yards and a tough, double-dogleg par-5 that first curves to the right and then bends back to the left. It roller coasters steeply uphill then back down and the left edge of the rough drops off dramatically, rolling a golf ball full speed to the out of bounds stakes. A pond sits in front of the green and requires a 60-yard **carry**.

"According to the scorecard," announced Franklin to Byron, "I need to give you a stroke here since my handicap is lower than yours. If I can make a par and you bogey this hole, we will be tied for the round." The duel was on!

Byron had the honors since he had birdied the last hole. Everyone became so quiet and still you could hear a duck quacking on a distant pond. He took a deep breath as he lined up his shot, assumed his address position and glanced one more time down the middle of the fairway just before he fired to a good finish position.

Whack! The ball was solid on the sweet spot of his driver, bore through the air and flew higher and higher with what seemed like an extra minute of hang time. The ball landed safely in the middle of the fairway about 260 yards away. "Wow!" exclaimed Byron. He had never hit the ball so well in his life and knew this was his career shot. He stood there still staring at the ball in shock.

Franklin stood in shock too. Byron had out driven Franklin many times, but what an opportune moment for a great shot! Franklin marveled to himself at how Byron put his best move on his tee shot. It was his turn next, and he kept his focus on a spot in the middle of the fairway. "Make a good solid swing and a good balanced finish," he thought to himself.

Smack! He watched the ball fly through the air with a slight fade, but it landed safely in the right center of the fairway. His tempo was a bit tentative as a result of still thinking about Byron's last shot, and his drive traveled only about 180 yards.

The foursome walked briskly to the forward tees. Karen already had a head start and was aligning her shot. She wondered for a moment how the new girl in the foursome ahead was doing. She hadn't played golf with her yet and didn't know whether she could beat her.

Suddenly, Karen walked away from her address position and started again while reminding herself she was only going to think about playing her personal best – down the middle and on the green in regulation. She made a beautifully smooth swing and the ball landed just where she had planned.

Amy could feel herself getting nervous. She recognized her Dad's red jacket as he watched from halfway down the fairway with some of the other parents. She wanted to do well for him. Everyone in the neighborhood knew he was a good golfer, and he had been so excited when she decided to play. She didn't want to disappoint him.

Just don't miss this shot, she thought to herself. She was nervous and topped the ball about fifty yards down the fairway. *Oh well*, she thought. *There's always the next tournament.*

She walked ahead to her shot since she was away and used a 5-wood. She hit a good shot down the middle. "Gee, it almost works better if I don't try," she thought.

Karen hit a slight hook into the left rough. "Don't go down the hill and out of bounds," she thought. The ball trickled just barely into the rough.

It was Franklin's turn. He began analyzing his shot as he walked up the fairway. "I like hitting a 7-iron into this green," he thought. "So I'll hit a 5-iron on this second shot and lay up to about fifteen yards short of the pond. That's enough to stay on the flat part of the fairway and not so close to the pond that I'll have a downhill lie. That will give me an easy 7-iron shot directly to the flagstick."

Franklin learned early in his golfing career always to plan one shot ahead so his next shot would be easier. He didn't always hit the ball well, but because he planned his shots in advance, his scoring average was usually surprisingly good.

The foursome finally arrived at Byron's tee shot. He began to think about hitting a 3-wood to the green and putting for eagle. He would have to clear sixty yards of water hazard on the fly. "Should I go for it?" he pondered. If he tried and succeeded, he might beat Franklin. After all, he just hit his career drive and even though he'd never made it to this green in two, he might just do it today.

Byron lined up his shot and fired. He hit another career shot! The ball kept flying and flying! "Get over! Get over!" he exclaimed. But the ball splashed two yards short of the far edge of the water hazard.

"Wow! You gave it a good try," exclaimed Franklin. He admired Byron's courage and his shot.

Byron made a mental note to himself. "Never try a shot you've never made before during a golf tournament."

Karen's golf ball was nestled in the deep grass in the left rough. She could barely see it. She could hit a 5-wood out of the rough and short of the hazard, but she was uneasy about how the ball was situated in the tall grass. She decided to hit an 8-iron back to the center of the fairway and then hit a 7-wood over the water and onto the green.

Amy hit a second 5-wood and landed short of the water hazard. She hit a 6-iron over the water as if she did this all the time and landed four feet to the right of the flagstick. She could hear her father cheering. "Way to go, Amy!"

Fortunately, the 18th green was large and the flagstick was situated in the center. The left side of the green is flat and the right side slopes toward the water hazard in front. Franklin hit a 7-iron as planned and landed pin-high and left of the flagstick by six feet on the flattest part of the putting surface.

Karen hit a 7-wood and landed on the green in line with the flagstick but short by eight feet. She was happy with this shot since putting uphill is easier than putting downhill.

Byron stopped short of the hazard, held out his arm and dropped another ball on the downhill part of the fairway sloping toward the water hazard. When he took his drop he was careful to keep the point at which the ball entered the hazard between where he dropped the ball and the flagstick. The ball landed three feet from the edge of the hazard when he dropped it. He selected a sand wedge, made a good swing but topped it, skimming the surface of the water and bouncing to the back edge of the green. He was now facing a difficult downhill putt that could possibly land him back in the water hazard.

Amy carefully pulled out the flagstick as everyone agreed they could see the hole with no problem. She placed a marker behind her ball and then fixed her ball mark. Franklin fixed his ball mark, marked his ball, and fixed Byron's ball mark for him since he was still walking to his ball. All three competitors were thinking about how this was the last putt of the round and crucial to the outcome of the tournament.

Byron mentally took into account his nerve-racking downhill putt, lined up, took his address and thought to himself, "Don't hit this too hard!" He gently tapped the ball and it began to roll slowly downhill, picking up speed with each roll. Everyone's eyes were following the ball as it kept rolling nearer and nearer to the hole. Byron's eyes lit up as he thought for a split second that the ball might roll in. He held his breath. The ball was rolling too fast, caught the rim of the hole and continued to roll five feet past the cup.

Karen putted next and sent a **lag putt** up to about six inches from the hole. She wanted to be careful not to end up past the cup and then have a testy two-footer downhill.

"Go ahead and putt out if you want," suggested Franklin. Karen tapped in her putt for an easy six. She hadn't been able to follow her plan to hit the green in regulation on the last hole, but she shot her best score ever. Later, she would learn she had won the Girl's Championship Division!

Franklin focused on his putt. It was an easy six-footer with a slight two-inch break to the right toward the water. Since Byron would at best double-bogey this hole, Franklin knew he could win if he made this birdie putt, even with giving Byron a stroke. But all he really cared about was that this would be a great birdie and he wanted to play this finishing hole to the best of his ability.

He made it! The gallery surrounding the green shouted and whistled. The clapping sounded like the loud roar of a lion. Franklin's knees felt weak from the pressure. He managed to pick up the ball from the hole and hold it in his fist. He pushed back the bill of his cap and stood watching Byron line up his putt, and let the game continue on as usual.

Byron sunk his five-footer. The crowd clapped as if to thank Byron for the great competition. He walked over to Franklin, shook his hand and smiled. "I'm going to keep practicing."

Amy was the last to putt. She had made it over the water and was putting for par.

The gallery was quiet again. She could not look up at the spectators or her father for fear she might get even more nervous. She made the putt!

She could hear her dad whistling over the applause. She felt her face turn red and she couldn't look up. She walked to the hole and picked up her ball. Karen returned the flagstick and gave Amy a congratulatory pat on the back.

To the gallery, Karen and Franklin were the winners of the tournament but all of the competitors knew they had all overcome greater obstacles than water hazards and bunkers. They had all won in their own way and little did they know at the time, but as they persevered, they were all to win more golf tournaments in the future.

Appendix

A Parent's Guide for the Beginning Golfer

Practice

Make sure all young beginners are supervised when playing and practicing. They don't realize there might be someone behind them when they are swinging a golf club, and they don't understand the damage that can be caused by a golf ball.

If a new golfer is fairly young, start with targets larger than the pyramid of golf balls. A large cardboard carton with a bull's eye drawn in the middle is fine.

The pyramid of golf balls is also fun to set up for putting with younger children. Set up several pyramids with designated areas to "tee off" from in a cleared area.

If a young beginning golfer is enthusiastic about wanting to go to the driving range and asks many times, provide a few individual golf lessons with a reputable teaching professional who has worked with kids. Bad habits form quickly with novices as they will figure out what works and use that as opposed to what will create better swing improvement in the future. This book is not meant to take the place of individual instruction nor is it by any means all you need to know about golf.

Group clinics and golf schools are a good way for beginning golfers to have fun and to see that not everyone hits great shots all the time.

Many new golfers are more comfortable taking a partial backswing at first. This may be because the club is too heavy or hard to control. They will soon develop enough coordination and strength to take a full swing.

On the Golf Course

When a new golfer can make dependable ball contact, it is time to try the golf course. Pick an easy, short course or a 9-hole par-3 course.

If a beginning player has never played on a course before, it is important to go with a friend or family member who is experienced.

With new players, feel free to tee up the ball in the fairway as well as on the teeing ground. New golfers who are not used to playing the ball "down" on the grass will find many shots difficult. Using a tee will also help the new golfer hit better shots with a better golf swing and more comfortably keep up the pace of play.

The first few times you play, have the new golfer use the same tees as the experienced player. After the new golfer takes a swing, pick up the ball and hit again from where the experienced player's ball lies. This is called a scramble format. Continue doing this until the ball is holed out.

As the new golfer improves, let them finish out their own ball from about thirty yards from the flagstick. Then increase the distance to fifty yards from the flagstick and so on.

Later let the beginner try hitting chip shots on the grass without a tee. When he/she can do this easily, then have him/her hit fairway shots without a tee. Always make goals and situations easy. The new golfer will develop better habits and have more fun.

Let kids enjoy hitting the ball. You'll see the excitement in their eyes when the ball gets airborne. Score may not be important for several years or ever at all.

Make sure you read Appendix II. This is very important for young golfers as well as adults.

Your Very Own Golf Clubs — Custom Club Fitting

Snow skiers make sure boots, poles and skis fit to give them their best performance. It is truly an advantage for golfers to make sure their equipment fits them for their best performance as well.

There are many design features to understand about golf clubs that influence the direction of ball flight. Here are some important considerations:

 Shaft Flex

Shafts can be made with different amounts of bend. Junior flex shafts have more whip to propel the ball into the air more easily for young golfers about twelve years old and younger. If shafts are too stiff, young golfers will compensate with grip positions that are not good but that will help get the ball airborne. This will promote bad habits that will be difficult to change later. Avoid cutting down adult shafts made for men or women. This will only make the club even stiffer.

If the shaft is too stiff the golfer will compensate with a poor grip.

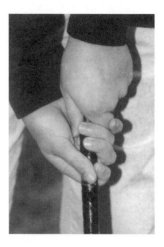

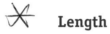 **Length**

If a young golfer has outgrown the length of a club, bad habits will ensue (for instance, the golfer's head bobbing up and down to get to the ball). The correct length will enhance a good, balanced swing and should be kept current with his or her growth.

Poor posture created by a club that is too short.

Better club length, better posture.

Loft

Most beginning students do not need a full set of golf clubs. Sometimes, a 7-wood, 7-iron, 9-iron, and putter are all that are necessary. These clubs have plenty of loft and will help young kids develop better balance. With longer clubs the new golfers resort to arm lifting and leaning on the back foot to get the ball airborne. Avoid low-lofted clubs like drivers, 3-woods, and 3-, 4-, and 5-irons.

Lifting the club for more loft will throw the swing off balance.

Lie Angle

The **lie angle** is the measure of angle from the sole as it rests on the ground to the angle of the shaft. If the lie angle is too flat for the golfer, only the toe of the club will touch the ground and the ball trajectory will be influenced to the right. Alternately, if the lie angle is too upright, the ball trajectory will be influenced to the left.

If the lie angle is too flat, the ball will go to the right of the target.

The correct lie angle will enable you to aim more accurately at the target.

If the lie angle is too upright, the ball will go to the left of the target.

The correct lie angle is best measured dynamically with a balanced golf swing using a **lie board**. A piece of tape is placed on the sole of an iron and a ball is placed on the lie board. When a good, balanced golf swing is made, the sole of the club will strike the ball and the board and a smudge mark will appear at the bottom of the sole. A good mark will appear near the middle of the sole under the sweet spot.

Because kids are still developing physically, the lie angle should be checked once a year, depending on how fast they grow. Since it is best to make sure the swing is being monitored and the full ball flight noted, it is very important that a teaching professional experienced in fitting golf clubs measures the lie angle.

Weight

Make sure golf clubs are not too heavy, particularly for very young golfers and those who are new to golf. A golf club may not seem heavy to pick up, but it becomes much heavier when creating momentum during a golf swing. If the club is too heavy, there will be a loss of balance and control. This is another good reason to avoid cutting down golf clubs made for adult men and women.

A club that is too heavy will create an off-balanced swing.

A swing that starts off-balance will end off-balance.　　*For a properly balanced swing, the clubs should be fitted to the golfer.*

The Grip or Handle

Rubber grips can be easily changed to different sizes and materials and most pro shops can provide this service at a fairly reasonable price. If the grip size is too big or too small it will affect grip tension. Grip size should be adjusted with the golfer's growth.

Grips should also be tacky. If they lose their tackiness, they either need to be cleaned or replaced. When grips become hard or smooth, it is very difficult to hold the handle and hit the ball well.

If clubs fit kids well, it will help them develop good technique so that they get the ball up into the air with better distance and accuracy. Golf will be much more fun.

Glossary

A Glossary of Golf Terms used in "The GolfBook for Kids"

Apron — the narrow area immediately around the green on which the grass is cut shorter than the fairway, but longer than the green.

Address position — the position a golfer takes when ready to hit the ball; address position includes stance, posture, orientation to the target line, and grip.

Away — farthest from the hole.

Back 9 — the second nine holes of an 18-hole course.

Backswing — the first part of the golf swing in which the golfer takes the club away from the ball and readies the club to hit the ball.

Ball-mark repair tool — a small device used to fix the indentation that a ball makes when the ball lands on the green.

Ball marker — a small token or coin used to show the exact placement of a ball on the green when the ball is picked up to be cleaned or moved out of the path of another ball.

Ball picker — the machine that is used to collect the golf balls at the driving range.

Birdie — a score in golf that is one stroke under par.

Bogey — a score in golf that is one stroke over par.

Break (of the green) — the way the golf ball turns as it rolls across the uneven surface of the green.

Bunker — a hazard on the golf course that is filled with sand.

Bunker shot — a shot taken to get a golf ball out of a bunker.

Caddie — a person whom you can hire to carry your golf bag and provide information about the course during a round of golf. The term caddie is an old, abbreviated form of the word "cadet" to denote a page employed by a knight.

Carry — the distance a ball has to fly in order to get over a hazard.

Casual water — a temporary accumulation of water on the golf course from which a golfer can remove a ball without penalty.

Chip shot — a short golf shot intended to get the golf ball onto the green; a chip shot generally flies about one third of the distance to the hole and rolls the rest of the way.

Course management — the process of planning shots and strategy to reduce risky shots and enable the golfer to hit the targets more successfully.

Course rating — a rating system that determines what a professional golfer would be likely to score on that golf course.

Cup — another name for the hole on the green in which the flagstick is located.

Dimples — the indentations on the surface of a golf ball that create air turbulence as the ball flies, thus giving the ball lift.

Divot — the clump of grass and dirt that is removed from the ground by a golf shot, and also the hole that remains.

Dogleg — a bend or turn in the layout of a fairway.

Draw — the flight of the golf ball when it curves slightly to the left after being struck by a right-handed golfer.

Driver — the 1-wood, usually used for teeing off on long holes.

Drop a ball — in a penalty situation or a relief situation, golfers may be required to place their golf ball back into play using specific rules that guide how to drop it.

Eagle — a score in golf that is two strokes under par on a hole.

Face — the front of the golf club that makes contact with the ball when the ball is struck.

Fade — the flight of the golf ball when it curves slightly to the right after being struck.

Fairway — the section of the golf course between the tee and the green in which the grass is mowed close.

Finish position — the end of the golf swing where the golfer's weight is over the front foot, hips are facing the target, and the end of the grip is also facing the target.

Flight — the levels of play in a tournament; the championship flight consists of the best players, while second or third flight include newer, less experienced players.

Follow through — the final part of the golf swing, from impact to the finish, in which the golfer turns toward the target and brings the hands up over the shoulders.

Fore! — the warning cry that is shouted by golfers to notify others that a golf ball is traveling toward them at high speed.

Forward swing — the part of the golf swing that starts at the top of the backswing and goes to the finish.

Front 9 — the first nine holes of an 18-hole course.

Getting on in regulation — hitting the golf ball onto the green in the number of shots required to leave two putts to make par (e.g., on a par three, landing the ball on the green in one shot).

Gimmie — a courtesy that golfers occasionally extend to one another in non-tournament play, by not making a golfer putt a very short putt that can easily be sunk — a golfer who gets a gimmie must still count the stroke it would have taken to sink the extra putt!

Golf ball — duh!

Golf etiquette — the code of proper behavior and courtesies that golfers extend to one another when playing on the golf course.

Green — the part of the golf course where the grass is cut the shortest, the surface has been specially prepared for putting, and on which the hole and flagstick are located.

Grip — 1) the special method of holding the golf club; 2) the material (usually a rubber like substance) that is wrapped around the handle of the club to allow the golfer to hold the club comfortably.

Handicap — a rating system for golfers to determine level of ability.

Handicap rating (for each hole) — a rating system for comparing the holes on the course for degree of difficulty (the #1 handicap hole is the most difficult on the course and the #18 is the easiest).

Hazards — places on the golf course that create problems for golfers in their efforts to reach the green.

Head — the business end of the golf club.

Heel — the part of the golf club at the base of the shaft and nearest to the golfer as the golfer addresses the ball.

Hole — the opening on the green, marked by the flagstick where golfers try to hit the ball.

Hole-in-one — getting the ball into the hole in one stroke.

Hole out — to hit the golf ball into the hole from on or off the green.

Honor — the privilege of going first on a hole after having gotten the best score on the previous hole.

Hook — the flight of the golf ball when it curves considerably far to the left after being struck.

Impact — the clubhead hitting the ball.

Irons — a set of golf clubs with slim, metal heads that are graduated in loft.

Lag putt — a long putt that serves to get the ball close to the hole so you can easily sink it on your next turn.

Lateral water hazard — a water hazard that usually runs parallel to the fairway; a golfer cannot easily drop the ball behind the hazard because it runs too far back.

Lay up — a course management technique used when a golfer cannot hit over a hazard in one shot. The golfer hits one short shot up to the hazard followed by an additional shot over the hazard (hopefully).

Lie — 1) the position of your ball on the ground as it pertains to the quality of the shot (with his ball in the fairway, he had a good lie); 2) the position of the ball on the ground as it pertains to how many shots had been taken to get it there (after two actual shots and one penalty stroke, a golf is said to "lie three").

Lie angle — the angle of the sole of the club in relation to the ground.

Linksland (Links) — the sandy, grassy terrain between the sea and the firm earth further inland. It was on the links that the game of golf evolved.

Lip — 1) the edge around the rim of the hole 2) the top edge of the bunker that often curls under.

Lipped out — a ball that went around the lip of the hole and rolled away.

Local rules — rules that pertain to a particular golf course; local rules may be in addition to the Rules of Golf or they may substitute for certain rules of the Rules of Golf.

Loft — the angle of the face of a golf club.

Lost ball — a ball that cannot be located after being hit in a round of golf.

Match play — the system of scoring a golf tournament in which golfers tally the total number of holes won by a golfer to determine the winner of the tournament.

Out of bounds — the area of a golf course designated to be beyond the playing area and marked by white stakes.

Overlapping grip — a method of holding a golf club in which the pinkie of the dominant hand rests on top of the index finger of the subordinate hand.

Par — the score an expert golfer would be expected to make on a given hole. Pars for different holes are designated according to their length: up to 250 yards is a par-3, between 251 and 470 is a par-4, over 470 is a par 5.

Pin — another name for the flagstick.

Pin-high — equidistant to the flagstick; a shot that travels the exact distance to the flagstick but is a bit to the right or left is said to be "pin-high."

Pitch shot — a moderately short golf shot intended to get the golf ball onto the green; a pitch shot generally flies about two thirds or more of the distance to the hole and rolls the rest of the way.

Pitching wedge — a golf club with more loft than a 9-iron that is designed to provide a high trajectory shot; generally marked with a "P" or a "PW."

Play through — to go past a group on the golf course.

Posture — the position of the golfer's body as the golfer addresses the ball.

Provisional ball — a ball played in place of one that may be lost.

Putter — a golf club with little loft that is designed to roll the ball to the hole.

Read the green — determine in which direction the ball will roll across the uneven surface of the green on its way to the hole.

Red stakes — markers on a golf course indicating which area is designated as a lateral water hazard.

Replace a divot — to put the piece of sod and grass, removed from the golf course by a golf shot, back into the spot from which it was removed.

Rough — the area of the golf course, generally running parallel to the fairway, in which the grass is allowed to grow longer than the fairway.

Rules of Golf — the set of rules, governed by the United States Golf Association and the Royal and Ancient Golf Club of St. Andrews, Scotland, that state the rules of play in a golf event.

Sand trap — another name for a bunker.

Sand wedge — a golf club with a high loft and a thick sole that is used to hit shots out of a bunker.

Score card — a card provided to golfers by the golf course for the purpose of the golfers keeping track of the scores for their round of golf; the score card usually also contains valuable information about the course including distances of holes, course ratings, and local rules.

Scratch golfer — a golfer who has a zero handicap.

Shaft — the long, thin part of the golf club that joins the head of the club to the grip, the flexibility of the shaft provides the extra "kick" that propels the ball forward.

Sky ball — a mis-hit golf shot that sends the ball very high in the air, but not very far in actual distance forward.

Slice — the flight of the golf ball when it curves considerably far to the right after being struck by a right-handed golfer.

Slope rating — a rating system for comparing golf courses to one another in degree of difficulty (a course with a slope of 125 would be more difficult than one with a slope of 118).

Sole — the base of the head of the golf club.

Stance — the overall body position of the golfer at the address of the golf ball.

Stroke — a forward movement of the club with the intention of hitting the ball (a swing and miss is counted as a stroke).

Stroke and distance — the penalty for an out of bounds shot in golf; the golfer must take a penalty stroke and hit again from the place where the ball was originally hit before it went out of bounds.

Stroke play — the system of scoring a golf tournament in which golfers tally the total number of strokes played through the entire round (or tournament) by the golfers to determine the winner of the tournament.

Summer rules — the regular Rules of Golf.

Sweet spot — the most solid place on the face of the golf club (lower middle) that, when hit, provides the most power to the ball and therefore the best shot.

Take away — the beginning of the golf swing in which the golfer first moves the clubhead back from the ball.

Target line — the imaginary line that runs through the golf ball straight to the point at which the golfer is aiming.

Tee — 1) the area on a golf course that is generally designated for hitting the initial shots on a golf hole; 2) a small wooden peg used to hold a golf ball up for purposes of hitting the ball.

Teeing ground — the area on a golf course between the tee markers and two club lengths back from the front of the tee markers, that is specifically designated for hitting the first shot on a golf hole.

Tempo — the pace at which a golfer swings a golf club.

Ten-fingered grip — a method of holding a golf club in which all of the fingers are directly on the golf club, similar to the grip used by a baseball player in gripping a baseball bat.

Tend the flagstick — to hold and remove the flagstick for other golfers in the group.

Through the green — refers to the whole golf course except the teeing ground, the putting green of the hole being played, and the hazards.

Touch (in putting) — the ability to hit a putt using the proper amount of force for the shot required.

Tournament rule sheet — the local rules governing a golf tournament.

Turn — the end of the front 9, going to the back 9.

Unplayable lie — the golf ball lands in a position from which the golfer cannot take a shot.

Water hazard — a designated body of water on the golf course (sea, lake, pond, river, ditch, surface drainage ditch, or open-water course), whether or not it contains water, marked by yellow or red stakes or lines from which the golfer may remove a ball with penalty strokes assessed.

Weight shift — the process of the golfer moving his or her weight through the ball as the swing progresses.

Whiff — a swing on which the golfer misses the ball (not a practice swing).

White stakes — markers on a golf course indicating which area is designated as out of bounds.

Winter rules – special rules, that because of poor grass conditions, allow golfers to pick up and clean a golf ball through the green and move it a short distance for a better lie.

Woods — 1) golf clubs with wooden heads or shaped to resemble the design of the traditionally wooden-headed clubs; 2) areas on the golf course with a dense growth of trees into which golfers would prefer not to hit their golf balls.

Wrong ball — a ball that is played that is not supposed to be played.

Yellow stakes — markers on a golf course indicating which area is designated as a water hazard.

Order Form

QTY.	Title	Price	Can. Price	Total
	The GolfBook for Kids **- Jim Corbett and Chris Aoki**	**$16.95**	**$21.95** **CN**	
	Shipping and Handling Add $3.50 for orders in the US/Add $7.50 for Global Priority			
	Sales tax (WA state residents only, add 8.6%)			
	Total enclosed			

Telephone Orders:
Call 1-800-461-1931
Have your VISA or
MasterCard ready.

INTL. Telephone Orders:
Toll free 1-877-250-5500
Have your credit card ready.

Fax Orders:
425-398-1380
Fill out this order form and fax.

Postal Orders:
Hara Publishing
P.O. Box 19732
Seattle, WA 98109

E-mail Orders:
harapub@foxinternet.net

Method of Payment:

☐ Check or
Money Order

☐

☐ MasterCard

Expiration Date: _____

Card #: _____

Signature: _____

Name _____
Address _____
City _____ State ____ Zip _____
Phone ( ) _____ Fax ( ) _____

Quantity discounts are available.
Call 425-398-3679 for more information.
Thank you for your order!